# IKEBANA

# IKEBANA

# The Art of Japanese Flower Arrangement

by *Georgie Davidson*
*in collaboration with*
*Beata Bishop*

New York and South Brunswick:
A. S. Barnes and Company

© 1967 by Georgie Davidson
A. S. Barnes and Co., Inc.
Cranbury, N.J. 08512
Printed in Great Britain
Library of Congress Catalog Card No. 67–10590

*TO BIG DA*
*LITTLE DA*
*AND TEDDY*

# Contents

*Chapter One*

# Ikebana - Its Origin, History and Philosophy

This book is about Ikebana, the Japanese art of flower arrangement. Literally Ikebana means "the arrangement of living material in water", and as a form of floral art it is entirely different from Western-style flower arranging.

The Western method produces floral decorations by using flowers for their colour effects in the same way as a painter uses his brush and palette. Ikebana, however, creates linear flower arrangements according to certain rules which aim at achieving perfect harmony, beauty and balance. One of its greatest Japanese exponents describes it as sculpture with flowers.

Ikebana is a unique way of creating beauty with plants, often with the addition of pebbles and small pieces of rock or wood which the Japanese regard as living parts of nature. At the same time it is also a way to achieve serenity, tranquillity and peace of mind. Unlike most hobbies and pastimes which engage only our minds through manual skill or imagination, Ikebana gently claims our whole personality, giving us, in exchange, equal parts of intellectual and emotional satisfaction. This claim may sound exaggerated, but only to those who have never tried their hands at this fascinating art.

Although Ikebana was virtually unknown in the Western world a mere twenty years ago, in Japan it has been in existence for fourteen hundred years. Like most art forms, it had its origin in religion, reaching Japan, together with Buddhism, in the sixth century. As in other lands and other religions, here, too, the temples became veritable art centres, promoting the development of architecture, sculpture, painting, literature, and, in Japan alone, flower arranging. According to legend, the Buddhist monks, to whom all life was sacred, used to gather the flowers and branches scattered by storms and arrange them in water-filled containers on their altars in order to keep them alive for a while. Called Shin-no-Nama – flowers of the God, i.e. Buddha – these salvaged plants were arranged with loving care by the priests. Much more than mere floral decorations, they served as an expression of veneration and worship.

This tender, reverent custom was the origin of Ikebana. It is an interesting fact that although most major religions have always made floral offerings to their gods, only the Japanese Buddhists succeeded in turning this custom into an independent art form. The first known person to have practised Ikebana was a Buddhist priest by the name of Ono-no-Imoko who lived in a lodge near a pond in Kyoto, and made flower arrangements in honour of Kuan-Yin, the Goddess of Mercy. Among the local people his home was known as Ike-no-bô, "the priest's lodge by the pond", and Ikenobo is also the name of the oldest flower-arranging school in Japan, still flourishing today under its forty-fifth Master who is a descendant of Ono-no-Imoko.

Ono-no-Imoko lived in the seventh century, but it was only in the fifteenth century that flower arrangement became a methodical art form and the subject of detailed treatises. At that time the range of available flowers was limited. Hard pressed by nature, the Japanese wasted no precious soil on cultivating flowers. That is why the earliest style, the Rikka or Rikkwa, consisted mainly of branches, grasses and perhaps a flower or two.

The Buddhist priests considered it important to give their arrangements a definite meaning. Early Rikka compositions were often designed to represent the universe in terms of plant material. The branches of pine, cypress, maple, bamboo and other trees and shrubs, nine different kinds in all, symbolized the mountains; the grasses stood for water, while the flowers represented the village and its cultivated fields.

Individual flowers also acquired symbolic meanings. For example the lotus stood for purity, sincerity and nobility, the iris for patriotism, the plum blossom, which in Japan breaks through the late winter snows, for courage. The pine symbolized longevity, the chrysanthemum immortality. The sight of pine trees, clinging to the rocky, windswept mountainside and braving the raging elements for centuries became associated with courage and a long life. All these wise, poetic symbols are still in use in Japan, so that while in a Western floral offering the message is stated on the enclosed card, in an Ikebana arrangement it is contained in the actual plant material. Once when my husband was ill, my Japanese teacher gave me a sansevieria plant for him. Seeing my surprise, she explained that the strong, straight leaves of the plant expressed her wish that my husband might soon grow strong and healthy again.

Standing in massive bronze containers, the early Rikka arrangements became ever bigger and heavier, often reaching a height of 10 ft. or more. They were formal, solemn and upward-looking, to meet the Buddha's eye from above. They also required much time and patience to arrange. By the time Rikka reached its greatest splendour, the art of flower arrangement had spread from the temples to the homes of noblemen and warriors who wished to adapt the art for domestic use. As a result the Shoka (or Seika) style was evolved. This, too, required heavy vases, but it was simpler and less formal than the original Rikka.

Most Westerners regard floral art as a feminine pastime. In Japan, however, Ikebana was evolved and practised by men – priests first, then warriors and noblemen – and although today millions of Japanese women practise it, men do so, too, and the great flower schools are almost invariably headed by men.

Indeed, in those early days the rapid progress of Ikebana from temples to private homes was due to those most masculine of men, the Japanese warriors who had discovered the soothing effects of flower arrangement and took to practising it between battles. Naturally, instead of transporting heavy bronze vases, the warriors improvised simple bamboo containers and used whatever plants they could find. All this made for greater simplicity. Later still, when Ikebana began to spread among the merchant classes, the more simplified Nageire, "thrown-in" style, came into existence.

The greatest and most revolutionary change came in the 1860s when Western culture, including Western flowers, first reached Japan. The resulting social and cultural upheaval had a great effect on Ikebana, too. The Flower Masters found it difficult to incorporate the exciting foreign flowers with their shorter stems and unfamiliar colours in the traditional arrangements; clearly a new approach was needed. And so, after a great deal of thought and consultation, the Moribana style was evolved by the Ohara School.

Moribana, "flowers heaped up", was radically different from the three earlier styles in so far as they required tall, upright vases, while Moribana introduced flat, shallow containers in which kenzans, i.e. pinholders, and heavy lead shippos kept the flowers and branches in position. This simple,

natural-looking style which is most suited to Western homes is also the most popular one outside Japan, and the style that captures more and more devotees in the Western world. Of course the term Ikebana embraces Rikka, Shoka, Nageire and Moribana, and several other styles which will be discussed later on. Amusingly enough, the modern approach to Ikebana is the exact reverse of its historical development. Throughout the centuries the art moved gradually from the highly formal temple style to its simpler, more relaxed varieties, and finally to the natural-looking Moribana. But Western students of the art reverse the process. They always start with Moribana which is the easiest; they then advance to Nageire, and only take up Shoka and finally Rikka after much advanced study and experience. According to Japanese Flower Masters, it takes about five years to train a competent Ikebana teacher; not a very long time compared with the fourteen-hundred-year history of the art.

Today Ikebana is more popular than ever in Japan. Hundreds of schools, thousands of qualified teachers and hundreds of thousands of students cultivate the art of floral arrangement in homes, schools, department stores and other public places. The old traditions live on side by side with ultra-modern developments, such as the free, modern, abstract and avant-garde styles which dispense with certain old rules and give great scope for individualism and self-expression.

The three most important schools in Japan agree on the basic principles of Ikebana but differ in matters of detail. The Ikenobo School, which is the oldest, teaches more Rikka and Shoka than the Ohara and Sogetsu Schools, which concentrate on Nageire, Moribana and contemporary styles. The Sogetsu School in particular is the one best adapted to the modern world of today. As a teacher of the Sogetsu School, I shall give its teachings pride of place in this book.

When it comes to breaking down international barriers and introducing Ikebana to the West, all schools find common ground in the modern style of flower arrangement based on the use of colour and design.

An old Japanese book says, "The study of floral art is a necessity for every man of culture, not only to develop the vigour of his mind but also to improve the kindly quality of his heart."

If this sounds too Oriental at first, let us see what Ikebana has to offer to the modern Westerner who knows little or nothing about Japan and Buddhism, and who is too harassed and busy to spend much time, thought or money on flower arrangement. What are the arguments in favour of Ikebana? To begin with the practical side, since the beauty of Ikebana depends on line, its economical use of plant material makes it a much cheaper method of beautifying one's home than the conventional type of Western floral decoration which depends on mass and volume.

The architectural structure and perfect proportions of Ikebana appeal to men who have a mathematical bent and to others who like to know how things are put together. It fascinates even those who do not normally notice floral decorations, however lavish. It is particularly appreciated by gardeners who hate to see their borders robbed of too many flowers.

Ikebana makes an ideal family hobby. Children can participate by looking for suitable pebbles, branches, driftwood and gnarled old roots during their walks and excursions. This makes them more aware of nature, and more careful in their handling of its materials. They learn never to pull up plants or hack off branches but rather to remove them carefully, without leaving a mark. As the most useful branches are normally found in low positions in the undergrowth, they can be removed without damaging or disfiguring the parent plant. In this way one learns to respect the economy of nature and of all living things, taking pride in never collecting more material than necessary.

Ikebana is a marvellous training for the eye, for the taste and for the skill of the arranger. As in all art forms, what you leave out is just as important as what you put in. The empty spaces between the components of your arrangement play as vital a rôle as the plant material. Since colours are subordinated to line and are used with restraint, Ikebana improves and refines the colour sense. What has begun as flower arrangement may eventually influence your whole way of life. Your growing ability to choose, compose and co-ordinate will affect your other activities. The lessons you learn from Ikebana are bound to bring a fresh approach to your choice of clothes and to the way you arrange your home. Ikebana trains you to seek perfection in line and colour, and to appreciate the simple, for it is simplicity which is the secret of grace and elegance in all things. By practising this art, you will come to appreciate the great Japanese respect for cleanliness. The water in your containers must always be pure and free from debris and sediment – you cannot tolerate stagnant water in your home – and your containers and pinholders must be scrupulously clean if your flowers are to last.

The special beauty of Ikebana arrangements must be experienced. These arrangements contribute to the atmosphere of the home much as would a fine painting or a piece of sculpture. Ikebana could well become a universal cultural asset to our daily lives because it is a creative art and a means of self-expression, so much so that Japanese experts claim to be able to read a person's character and mood from his or her flower arrangement. It is the only floral art that combines supreme elegance with the appearance of natural life and growth.

The study and practice of this art requires self-discipline which helps the development of one's character. Working and co-operating closely with nature in making a floral arrangement should give one a sense of humility and truth, while the joy of producing a thing of beauty satisfies the creative urge which, in most of us, is ever present, but too often latent.

Last but not least, Ikebana is a natural tranquillizer. Although even in Japan it has lost most of its religious character, it has retained all its spiritual beauty and serenity. However depressed and miserable you may feel, the moment you start a floral arrangement the need for concentration and the handling of living, natural materials miraculously takes your mind off your worries and anxieties. Your problems recede, and when you have finished your arrangement, the satisfaction of having created harmony and beauty makes you feel relaxed.

When it comes to relieving tension and acquiring a feeling of serenity, Ikebana is better than any drug. The only characteristic it shares with drugs is that it is definitely habit-forming. In Ikebana circles it is generally agreed that when everything goes wrong, the best remedy is to shut oneself away and start making a floral arrangement. Some people maintain that the quickest way to get rid of a black mood is to produce a tormented "black" arrangement, but it is probable that even if you set out to do so, you will actually produce a tranquil one instead and emerge in a more peaceful state of mind. Being still, concentrating hard and occupying oneself with the basic realities of pure line, space, balance and proportion is a marvellous panacea.

The tranquillizing effect of Ikebana on sick people is impressive. Once when my husband was ill in hospital, I made a simple arrangement for him. A walking patient came into his room, saw the flowers and insisted on taking them to the main ward. The sister approved of the idea so much that she left the arrangement on the centre table all the time and even put it under the night-light for the benefit of restless patients. After that first occasion, every time I visited the hospital I went prepared to make two arrangements, one for my husband, one for the ward. It seemed to interest the patients and heighten their morale.

Not long ago a class of occupational therapy students to whom I had given a lecture decided to form an Ikebana study group. They realized that this floral art would be a great help to their patients. And I myself witnessed the gradual recovery of a woman who, after a severe nervous breakdown, found strength and a new, positive outlook on life through the study and practice of Ikebana.

It is said that no one who has acquired even the slightest knowledge of this art would willingly go back to his previous state of ignorance, because even that little knowledge has changed his outlook on, and appreciation of, nature. Once the basic rules of Ikebana have been understood, one cannot walk through a garden without seeing plant patterns everywhere, or making imaginary flower arrangements.

*A selection of kenzans, with straightener, and shippos.
On the right, basic tools include knife
with two cutting edges, springless shears, hand-saw,
syringe and small hatchet*

# Chapter Two

# The Practical Approach: Equipment, Care and Treatment of Material, and Choice of Containers

Like all other arts, Ikebana has its essential tools and basic rules. Once you have mastered these, you will find work both easy and enjoyable.

Tools first. You need a small tool kit, specially made for the purpose in Japan and sold in this country. Compact in a neat leather or beautiful brocade case, it contains the following equipment:

1  A pair of springless shears which allow you to work without tensing your muscles. Shears are made in three different sizes. Eventually you may wish to own all three for different purposes. Keep them well oiled and clean at all times.

2  A combined pump and spray used to inject water into the cellular stems of lotus flowers, water lilies, and their leaves which would otherwise wilt, and to spray the finished arrangement.

3  A light saw to cut thick branches. This is also used in the wedging technique which is described in the basic rules.

4  A knife with two cutting edges for trimming thick branches and splitting woody stems.

5  A small chopper to cut gnarled old ivy from trees, and to shape the base of heavy, strong branches for placing in the appropriate holder.

These tools are used in making arrangements in all styles. But as Western students always start with Moribana, our next concern is the kenzan or pinholder.

There are many sizes and shapes of kenzans, with pins of different lengths, diameters and densities. You will build up your collection as you go along. Whatever the type, it must be of top quality: sufficiently heavy, with strong brass pins which do not rust, bend or loosen after the first use. To buy a cheap kenzan is economy of the worst kind. True, there is a special tool for straightening bent pins, but even that is of little help with an inferior kenzan. The beginner's first kenzan should have medium-length, close-set pins for general purposes. The next one should have a shippo in the centre for holding thick branches. Before the invention of the kenzan, the shippo was the only Moribana holder, made of lead and often shaped like a crab, tortoise or honeycomb.

Kenzans with longer pins are used to hold fleshy stems. There is also the well kenzan, a pinholder with its own tiny water container which can be used on its own, without a separate container, and the combined sun-and-moon kenzan for divided arrangements. Minute kenzans are used in floating arrangements to support invisibly the heads of individual flowers.

A kenzan should never be obtrusive. It may be seen but should not be conspicuous when the arrangement is viewed from a distance of three feet. It is a good idea to paint kenzans – with special paint which does not harm plant life – so that they will blend better with the containers. For dark ones the kenzan should be painted dark green; for light ones, white. In a large container you can conceal the kenzan by placing a piece of driftwood or some attractive pebbles in front of it, piling them up in a casual fashion and tailing them off in a tadpole shape. Camouflage is also possible by inserting a downward-sloping leaf at the front. The Japanese word for such concealing materials is *tomi*. According to a much-quoted rule, your *tomi* should never turn into *gomi*, i.e. a scrap heap. You should certainly never put anything in the water that is likely to decay quickly. If two kenzans are used in one container, conceal them with two informal piles of pebbles, leaving some room in between. This is known as the Goldfish Path – a charming gesture of courtesy towards imaginary fish which may wish to inspect the arrangement.

Next come the containers. For Moribana, containers must be flat and shallow, with an average depth of 2 to 3 in. They can be rectangular, triangular, oval, curved or irregularly shaped. There are no hard and fast rules about choosing them, provided that the container is used as an integral part of the arrangement, and its size, colour and texture harmonize with the flowers, the season and the setting of the arrangement.

At first it is best to choose simple pottery shapes in earthy colours – browns, greys, dull blues – which

A selection of classical and modern containers

blend easily. As the container symbolizes the soil, earthy colours are a natural choice for it.

A charming Ikebana tradition decrees that containers should be attuned to the seasons, just as a truly elegant person matches her clothes and accessories to the time of year. Metal containers are recommended for winter, pottery ones for spring and autumn, while summer flowers look best in a basket container suitably lined to hold the water.

As opposed to Moribana, the upright Nageire calls for tall containers, ranging from traditional bronze bases to modern pottery shapes. A rough inside texture makes arranging easier by helping to keep the branches in position.

Boat-shaped and moon-shaped containers and baskets are common to both styles.

Containers are often put on bases, called *dai* in Japanese, partly to protect polished surfaces, partly to complete the outline of the arrangement. The classical Japanese base is a flat piece of black polished wood with scroll ends. Many other varieties are also used. They are always required for classical arrangements, and often for natural and free-style ones. Modern, abstract and avant-garde arrangements rarely stand on bases; neither do basket containers. The proportion of base to container must be consistent with the particular arrangement. Obviously no one would place a large container on a tiny base. But a small container on a large base creates a pleasant impression of spaciousness, providing balance is maintained by placing a few stones, a piece of wood or some leaves outside the container.

*A selection of containers. Left to right: salt-glaze stoneware, modern black ceramic, tall cream stoneware, square black, Scandinavian glass, old English coffin bottle, and two dark salt-glaze containers*

The well pinholder, mentioned among the different kinds of kenzan, always stands on a base, suitably camouflaged by pebbles or a twisted root.

So much for equipment. The most important component, however, is the plant material which you wish to preserve. Ikebana lore, handed down through generations, enables you to achieve the best results. If you grow your own flowers, choose those which have not yet reached full maturity, and cut them before sunrise or after sunset. Carry a bucket of cold water and put the flowers in it up to their necks as soon as you have cut them, and leave them for at least an hour. Do the same with branches and leaves. This process is known as conditioning. When you cut wild flowers or branches during a country walk, wrap their ends immediately in a clean handkerchief or some paper. It is even better to wrap them up completely in sheets of newspaper. On no account carry the plants in your bare hand. All else failing, tie a loop of string around the stems and use it as a handle. Try to protect the plants from sunshine and strong wind. As soon as you get home, unwrap the plants and hold them upside down in a bunch under a slowly running cold tap. Then wrap them in paper, sprinkle them again and lay them in a cool, dark place. This will revive them amazingly. Flowers sold by good florists have been conditioned. But, like all other plants, they too should be left in deep water in a cool place for some time before being arranged. Wipe clean the leaves of evergreens to give them an attractive gloss.

The simplest and most effective way to prolong the life of cut flowers is to cut about an inch off their stems under water just before arranging them. Do this with the aid of a bowl full of cold water. Immerse both the ends of the stems and the shears, making your cut at least $1\frac{1}{2}$ in. below the water surface. This prevents the formation of an air-lock which would stop the flower from drawing up fresh water; the pressure enables the flower to draw up more water. This treatment is called Mizu-giri. Some plants need more help than this universally useful life-prolonging process. Singeing or "boiling" the ends of stems, or dipping them into certain chemical substances will preserve the life and looks of plants, provided that they are fresh and strong to begin with.

Before using chemicals, make sure that they will not ruin the inside of the container. If you do not take this precaution, you may lengthen the life of a three-shilling bunch of flowers, but ruin a valuable silver entrée dish.

Whatever chemical treatment you use, arrange the flowers and then leave them without water for a few minutes, otherwise the benefit of the treatment will be lost.

Cleanliness is the best life preserver. Keep your containers and pinholders spotless. Tolerate no leaves or broken stems in the water; they decay rapidly, creating impurity. A lump of charcoal in the container helps to keep the water fresh, but even so you must change the water frequently – every other day in spring, daily in summer when the water gets warmer and bacteria breed faster. Old, stale water is useless and even harmful to flowers.

The less you handle your cut plants the better. Treat fragile ones with special care. Camellias, for instance, should have their sensitive heads wrapped in tissue paper before being handled, and should be sprayed afterwards with mildly salty water to prevent discoloration.

Remember, the life expectation of all cut plants depends on their ability to absorb water. That is why their area of absorption must be increased. In the case of tough, woody stems this is done by splitting and cutting the end at an angle. With all flowers it helps to leave a leaf near the flower head, since this acts as a natural water pump.

*Plant Preservation Methods*

*Singeing:*

Hydrangeas, magnolias, poppies, rhododendrons, maple leaves and all plants that yield a milky juice when cut benefit from having the base of their stems singed in a flame. Before doing this, wrap paper round the flower heads to protect them from the heat.

*Boiling:*

Dahlias, roses and godetias will last longer if you plunge their cut stems for a couple of inches into boiling water for a few seconds and then put them in deep, cold water.

*Chemical methods:*

1 Oil of peppermint. Buy this in small quantities from the chemist and transfer it into a squat jar with a sufficiently wide neck which allows you to dip in the flower stems. The jar should have a plastic top. Do not leave the stems in for more than 2 or 3 seconds; misguided generosity will kill your flowers instead of prolonging their lives. Flowers which benefit from this treatment are these:

| | |
|---|---|
| *Acacia* | *Honeysuckle* |
| *Aster* | *Hosta* |
| *Balsam* | *Inula christii* |
| *Bougainvillea* | *Jasmine* |
| *California poppy* | *Loosestrife* |
| *Canna lily* | *Mallow* |
| *Caryopteris* | *Mesembryanthemum* |
| *Chinese bell flower* | *Periwinkle* |
| *Chrysanthemum* | *Poppy* |
| *(for leaves)* | *Snapdragon* |
| *Dahlia* | *(antirrhinum)* |
| *Deutzia* | *Solomon's Seal* |
| *Flax* | *Spiraea* |
| *Foxglove* | *Tamarisk* |
| *Gardenia* | *Trachelospermum* |
| *Gentian* | *jasminoides* |
| *Geranium* | *Wistaria* |
| *Gerbera* | *Yarrow* |
| *Gloxinia* | *Zinnia* |

2 Powdered alum. Keep this handy in a small pot with a deep lid. Sprinkle some into the lid and dip in it the stems of maple leaves and canna lilies which would otherwise tend to wilt.

3 Caster sugar. Dip the cut stems of tulips into this immediately before arranging, to stop them from undulating.

Once you have your equipment ready and your plant material in condition, you can start thinking about your first arrangement. And the very first thing to decide is where your arrangement is to stand. This is vital. To do the reverse, namely to make the arrangement and then begin to wonder where to put it, is asking for failure.

There is nothing surprising about this. People go to endless trouble to find the best and most harmonious way to arrange their furniture; placing an Ikebana arrangement deserves the same care. For one thing, the arrangement must be placed where it can be seen to best advantage; for another, it must be in tune with its surroundings. This means that if, for instance, the arrangement is to stand on a low or average-height table, the angle of the flowers must rise towards the spectator. But if it is to be displayed at or above eye level, on a tall shelf or in a hanging container, they must be focused downwards, descending towards the onlooker without any suggestion of drooping.

Nothing enhances a beautiful arrangement more than a plain background. If the position of your choice happens to be against a patterned wallpaper or a shelf full of distracting objects, hang a piece of plain fabric on a bamboo rod behind it, thus making a Kakemono.

Next, choose your container, bearing in mind the plant material you wish to use. Normally the more conservative the container, the more smoothly it will fit in with the rest of the furnishings. As mentioned in the previous chapter, seasons have some bearing on the containers used, but, if in doubt, choose a simple one in an unobtrusive colour.

Observing the seasons is one of the great joys of Ikebana. Even to an air-conditioned artificial urban existence where there is nothing to remind one of the rhythm of the year, Ikebana suddenly restores the mood and ambience of nature's changing seasons. Spring and summer bring a multitude of seasonal flowers. Autumn is best expressed with foliage, seed pods and berries. Winter calls for beautifully shaped bare branches, moss and driftwood, sparingly used to suggest dormant nature. There are many variations on these basic themes. In the windy month of March, for instance, you can give your branches exaggerated curves to suggest the turbulence of the air outside. At the grim tail end of winter the addition of a spray of flowering cherry or a budding camellia to a bare, austere arrangement expresses the first stirring of spring. On a hot summer's day a single bloom, sprayed with water as if dripping with dewdrops, looks delightfully cool.

In the subtle language of Ikebana even the expanse of water visible in the flat Moribana container has a meaning of its own. In summer, water is cooling; in winter, chilling. Therefore in summer you place your arrangement at the back of the container, leaving plenty of water visible; in winter you put it at the front to show less water.

This is the moment to stress an important point. In Moribana the kenzan holding the flowers can be placed in many positions within the container, but only in classical arrangements does it occupy the centre. Nature rarely produces strict symmetry, and neither should your arrangement, a re-creation of nature, show too much regularity.

Remember the seasons when handling your plant material, especially with regard to the sap in the branches. Spring branches full of rising sap are easier to shape than are dry, dormant ones. The soft new growth of early summer must be treated very carefully.

Nature provides you with raw material which you must "process" before starting to arrange it. This consists of trimming and shaping. As you will see in the following chapter, the respective lengths of your branches and flowers are highly important, for they must be in proportion to the container and to each other. So let us first make ourselves familiar with the rules of cutting, trimming, and shaping.

The branches will come first. These have been cut from trees or shrubs in the woods or garden. Now you must adapt them to the smaller proportions of your room by removing some laterals and leaves.

Look at your branch from the back. This makes it easier for you to see its structure. Often the tip is weak. Once you have decided what length you need – according to the rules in the next chapter – you may wish to measure this length from the base upwards and dispense with the weak tip altogether.

Remove damaged and broken leaves, weak, dry twigs, and, in natural arrangements, all leaves and laterals that cross each other or a main stem. Sometimes a branch has a particularly elegant line which can be emphasized by removing the leaves from one side only. The knowledge of what to remove and what to leave can only be acquired through practice, but if you give your whole mind to it, progress will be quick. The line of your branch is your best guide. Always cut the base of the branch at an angle so that the cut will be uppermost when you put the branch in position on the kenzan. Not only is it easier to cut slantwise across the fibrous tissue, but the resulting shape will go more readily on to your pinholder.

Thin branches can be easily cut with shears. So can thick ones, thanks to a special technique which saves your shears from ruin and the muscles of your hand and arm from tension, while also keeping the bark of the branch undamaged.

This is how you do it. Holding the branch in your left hand, decide the angle at which it will be placed. Hold the shears in your right hand, tips on top. As there is a correct way of holding and playing musical instruments, there is also the right way to hold the shears. The small curve at the shears' ends should touch your palm. Open the shears with your index finger. Mark the bark where the cut is to be. Turn the branch upside down. With the back of your right hand to the branch, clamp the shears around the mark. Hold the branch firmly with your left hand, then lift the shears away to the right. For a very tough branch you will need two or three "lifts", but not much force. While cutting, your elbows should be tucked in at your sides.

Now that your branch is the right length, you start shaping it to conform to the correct angles, as explained in the next chapter. Shaping is done by simultaneous twisting and bending. To bend without twisting is largely a waste of time. Even if you give your branch a graceful, arching line, it will straighten itself as soon as you put it in water. Hold the branch between your thumbs and index fingers, one thumb being on top, the other one, opposite, on the underside. Bend it in the desired direction, twisting gently at the same time until you feel that the inner skin is giving way. Continue in the same manner at intervals along the branch as necessary, taking care not to break it, and always bending between the nodes.

The same technique is used on laterals, though more gently. Laterals are tender. So are the joints where the leaves grow from the main stem. Fold the leaves into your palm before bending and twisting, to avoid bruising them. Sometimes individual leaves need twisting and bending too, to make them turn upwards in the "happy position", or to correct an imperfect line. Touch the leaves gently as if they were butterflies' wings. Support them with one hand where they join the branch while twisting and bending their supple green stems with the other.

The twisting and bending method can be used on all branches up to the thickness of a pencil. For thicker ones Ikebana teaches the wedging method which is both simple and ingenious.

Having decided the way you want your thick branch to bend, make a cut with your handsaw to approximately one-third of the total thickness on the top side. Gently bend the branch over your finger to give it support, gradually opening the cut and inserting in it a tiny wedge which you have previously cut from the base. It is important to use wedges from the parent branch, partly because their colour will blend, partly because their consistency and sap contents will match those of the branch. Depending on the curve you want to achieve, put in wedges at intervals of an inch or so until you get the desired shape.

No visible trace of trimming must remain. Camouflage all cuts and marks on the branch with ink or charcoal. In the finished arrangement the bark must look intact. To shape branches which are too thick for ordinary bending and twisting but not thick enough for wedging cut them, on the underside, at a slant of 45°

to one-third of their thickness in a few well-chosen spots, and, holding firmly, twist and bend them. In this way there will be enough undamaged bark left for the branch to draw up water. This method is often used when cutting the "oars" for boat arrangements.

All branches are placed firmly on the kenzan in an upright position and then slanted in the required direction.

On the other hand always cut flower stems straight across and place them on the kenzan at the required angle. Beware of letting all your flower heads face the same way. To use the Japanese approach, the flowers must be grouped as if they were chatting with each other, but never to the extent of turning their backs on the spectator.

If your flower stems are too thin to stay in place on the kenzan, you are probably using the wrong pinholder for the job, but even so the trouble is easy to cure. Wrap the end of the stem in a small piece of paper, or push it into a short length of drinking straw or a hollow stem you may find among the debris. If your flower has a hollow stem, insert a twig or sliver of bamboo as a supporter.

For a heavy branch which may topple over, cut a short supporting stick at the same angle and use it as a prop, to take some of the weight.

Incidentally, give some thought to the balance of the kenzan itself while arranging flowers. The weight of the kenzan goes some way towards keeping it steady, but it is good sense to insert your materials first in the middle and then at positions near the edge. If your heaviest branch slants to the left, use the kenzan as a counterpoise by turning it slightly to the right to effect balance, and vice versa.

Calla lilies have the bad habit of curling their stems at the base which makes fixing awkward. Counteract this by making a collar of short twigs or straight stems around the base of each lily, or bind it with bass. This stops it from curling up, besides serving as a support. Ikebana is full of ingenious little hints like these, which is why artificial aids like plasticine or chicken wire are not used.

However skilled you become in shaping plant material, don't overdo it. We must respect nature sufficiently not to interfere with the characteristic growing habits of plants. There is no harm in bending willow twigs for instance, because they are flexible by nature. Indeed, they are often made to form a boomerang-shape in arrangements made for a leave-taking, because in symbolic language this means "come back soon". It would, however, be quite wrong in a natural arrangement to try to bend or shape the stems of irises or bulrushes which are straight and upright by nature.

When in doubt, consider the natural growing habits of plants and be guided by them.

# Chapter Three

# The Sogetsu School of Ikebana, Its Brief History and Teaching Pattern

Of the many hundreds of Ikebana schools in Japan, three are world famous, and among these the Sogetsu School of Japanese flower arrangement is one of the largest and most modern in technique and outlook. It was started in 1926 by Sofu Teshigahara, the present Grand Master, who is the son of a famous teacher of a classical school. Mr Teshigahara began his Ikebana training at the age of seven. As he grew older, he realized that in a changing world Ikebana must either adapt itself to present-day conditions or stagnate and die. So he started the necessary reforms, and after many years of untiring effort and hard work he succeeded in setting a new trend, taking the best from the old, and incorporating in it much that was new.

Sofu Teshigahara is not only a man of great artistic ability – he is a well-known painter and sculptor – but also a sound workman. What he started amidst much opposition in 1926 is today a growing, thriving and inspiring school, with an ever-increasing following in the Western world. The Sogetsu School was the first to make use of such apparently unpromising material as glass, vinyl, plaster of Paris and iron. Although it is a progressive school, eminently adapted to modern requirements and the possibilities of the Western home, it also teaches the more formal classical arrangements.

What appeals most to the Occidental student is the logical sequence of the Sogetsu teaching pattern. Although the early instructions may at first seem rigid, full of do's and don'ts, the only set rules are for the positions and angles of the main branches; the rest is no more than suggestions to aid you in the early stages of your work. As you progress and master the fundamentals, even the set rules may be relaxed and ultimately disregarded, but not before they have achieved their object. In Ikebana, as in everything else, it is a fatal mistake to try to run before learning to walk.

To quote Mr Teshigahara, "It will be entirely wrong to think that the Sogetsu School is so free as to admit the title of Ikebana to self-styled haphazard works. I should, therefore, venture to say that these haphazard arrangements should be called pseudo-Ikebana. Those who have an ardent desire to create something free, beautiful and attractive, must think sincerely of the most effective methods to improve their skill. The various phases of the flowers and trees and their intimate beauty which is variable according to seasons, the abundant ideas of the worker, and the beauty of the vessels and environment – the Ikebana of the Sogetsu School must be a combination of these three elements."

In the old days of leisure and adequate domestic help it was possible to spend years sitting at the feet of a teacher, and devote a whole day to making an arrangement. Today this is impossible both for the Oriental and the Occidental flower arranger. The teaching pattern of the Sogetsu School fits in admirably with the less leisurely lives we lead today. I myself had the good fortune to receive my senior training from a very logical and firm teacher. Mrs Fujitsuka of the Sogetsu School was in London for the period of her husband's appointment only, and she made her conditions for accepting me as a pupil very clear. "My time is limited," she said. "I have no time to waste. If you wish to be well trained, you must come to my house. If you say that you must go home before you have done good work, I will say, 'Go. And don't come back'." This sounded most un-Oriental, but it was effective, and she certainly was a wonderful teacher. The teaching pattern of my school in London is based on the principles Mrs Fujitsuka taught me.

To illustrate this book I have photographed mainly natural-style arrangements, for I believe that it is wrong to study the modern, free, abstract and avant-garde styles through the work of one person only. Besides, as the camera has only two dimensions, a great deal is lost in photographs. I myself have for many years studied the photographs of Free Style exhibition pieces in various Sogetsu books, and although I found them interesting, I had no true conception of their size and magnificence until I saw an exhibition in Berlin for which no fewer than five gigantic arrangements had been made by the Grand Master himself.

A successful Free Style exhibition arrangement is the zenith in Ikebana. But just as it would be foolish for an inexperienced climber to try to scale the north face of the Eiger, common sense and humility tell us that until we have learnt and mastered the rudiments of design, we should not attempt publicly to make these arrangements. However, in the seclusion of a workshop or garden, trial and error are invaluable teachers.

Arrangements can be divided into three classes – those made for the home, those for study groups, and those for exhibitions. All three are different by nature and fulfil different requirements. Of course we are primarily concerned with arrangements made for our own homes which are meant to beautify our surroundings and create focal points of serenity and loveliness, in keeping with the mood and atmosphere of their environment. Such arrangements are the very heart of Ikebana.

Let us first concentrate on the fundamentals. Your first steps are guided by instructions and carefully designed diagrams, giving both the elevation and bird's-eye view of each arrangement. The former gives you the angles, and the latter the positions of the main lines. Both are important, but the bird's-eye view is the more helpful of the two.

In our arrangements we use three main lines. It pays to learn their Japanese names and symbols, since these constitute a kind of international Ikebana language which you may find useful in the future. I certainly did when I taught in Germany not long ago, and although my German is of schoolgirl standard, my students and I had no linguistic difficulties at all in Ikebana matters.

The first branch, which is the longest of the arrange-

ment, is called Shin, or Heaven. The second branch is called Soe, or Man, and the third Hikae, or Earth. It is on this principle of three that all Ikebana arrangements of the Sogetsu School are based. The symbol for Shin is a circle, for Soe a Square, and for Hikae a triangle. These are used in all our diagrams.

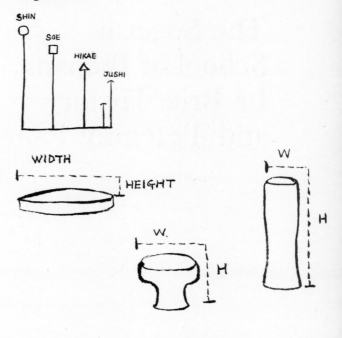

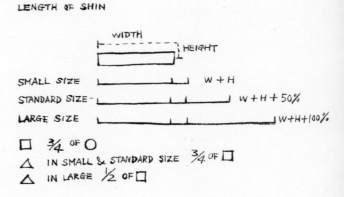

To accommodate the variety of material provided by nature, we have a choice of three measurements for Shin – small, standard, and large. The small measurement equals the diameter of the container plus its height. The standard size equals the diameter of the container plus its height plus 50%. The large size is the diameter plus the height plus 100%. Soe is in all cases three-quarters of Shin. Hikae, in the small and standard sizes, is three-quarters of Soe, and in the large size half of Soe.

Any additions to the three main lines are called jushi, or supplementaries. A jushi can be a flower, a leaf, a branch or a root; it is a supporter, and as such it should never dominate, its length must be not more than two-thirds the length of the main line it supports. In view of the proportion of Soe to Shin, a supporter to Shin can be as long as Soe, so we must be very careful to place it supporting Shin,

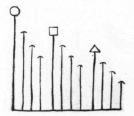

otherwise it would make a pair with Soe. And this, being symmetrical, would not be acceptable, since there is very little symmetry in nature. The only logical symmetry in nature is that of two eyes, ears, legs, or arms, or even twins, for which the Greeks, those supreme logicians, used the dual number instead of the plural. In Oriental art no two components of a pair are ever precisely alike. The symbol for jushi is a T-shape.

In the Sogetsu School we have two types of arrangement, Moribana and Nageire. Moribana literally means "piled up"; the term is used to describe an arrangement in a shallow container where a kenzan or shippo is used. The literal meaning of Nageire is "thrown in"; it is an arrangement in a tall container, the main lines being kept in position by a kubari, a fixing made of natural materials.

Arrangements fall into the natural, free style, classical, modern, abstract and avant-garde categories.

Finally there are two styles, the Upright and Slanting Style. The Japanese term for the upright is Risshin Kei. The Slanting Style is divided into three sections: the Keishin Kei, or Slanting Style, the Haishin Kei, or Flat Style, and the Suishin Kei, or Hanging Style. It is the position of Shin, the longest branch, which determines the style of the arrangement. In the Sogetsu School all angles are measured from an imaginary zero line which rises vertically from the centre of the kenzan in a Moribana arrangement, or from the centre of the neck of the tall container in a Nageire arrangement. It is important to remember that the imaginary zero line is not vertical in all schools. In some it is horizontal, and this can create confusion in one's mind if one is watching an Ikebana demonstration and it is not made clear from which line the angles are measured.

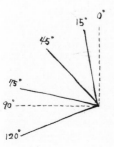

According to the Sogetsu rules, which we shall follow, in the Upright Style Shin, the longest branch, is always at an angle of $5°-15°$ from the imaginary vertical zero line. In the Slanting Style the tip of Shin is always at an angle of $45°$. In the Flat Style it is between $75°$ and $85°$, and in the Hanging Style between $110°$ and $130°$. The horizontal rim of the container represents an angle of $90°$, which means that the tip of Shin at $110°-120°$ will be below it. It cannot be sufficiently emphasized that it is the tip of the branch which must be at the correct angle. The base of the branch may rise from the kenzan, shippo or kubari at a different angle; it would be a very dull arrangement if all branches were completely straight; but it is the position of the tip that matters. In Moribana arrangements there are six positions for the kenzan in the container: left front, right front, right rear, left rear, centre front and centre rear.

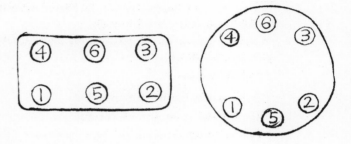

Using the correct positions adds variety to the arrangements and makes the placing of the plant material easier. The general rule is that for a left-hand arrangement, in which the branches go to the left, we use a right-hand position, and vice versa. There are exceptions to this rule which will be mentioned in the appropriate context.

Try to memorize the kenzan positions by their numbers on the diagram, so that you automatically associate No. 1 with left front, for example, No. 6 with centre rear, and so on. This will save you much time and trouble later on.

The space known as the Pool of Thought supplies the accent on space which, we are taught, is as vitally important in Ikebana arrangements as the accent on line. The name itself suggests a focus of tranquillity which aids contemplation and radiates quiet serenity; indeed, the Pool of Thought, which always lies between two main lines, must be kept free and open, just as thoughts should never be encircled or intruded upon. The correct space for the Pool of Thought is given in the instructions.

The Sogetsu School has fifty rules for the student to consider before starting on his or her first arrangement. Here are some of the most important ones:

"Although flowers are beautiful, all flower arrangements are not always admired."

"A proper flower arrangement is acceptable in any kind of life and at any time of life."

"The true spirit of flower arrangement is changeless, but styles of arrangement can be varied according to circumstances or surroundings."

"Give an accent to one blossom or one branch when you arrange flowers."

"Talk to flowers."

"Don't worry about your results."

"Be pure, be calm and be careful."

"The main plants form the bone structure of the arrangement, and the minor ones add flesh to it."

"When making an arrangement, consider the relation between the flowers and the container."

"Placing Hikae is more difficult than placing the other two main branches, so take great care with it."

"Proportion and harmony are more important than the number of plants used."

"The smallest and largest flowers are equally valuable for Nageire."

"Much skill is required for arranging flowers freely and naturally while observing the basic principle."

"Create harmony between flowers, containers and the room."

"Avoid the repetition of similar lines; make accents."

"An ornate container calls for a simple arrangement."

"Train your eyes to grow appreciative and your hands to become creative, and make constant efforts to improve your skill."

Before starting on an arrangement you must make certain decisions which will, with practice and experience, become easy and automatic.

1 Choose the place where your finished arrangement is to stand. This will make a great deal of difference to the angles and positions of your branches, and therefore to the style of your arrangement, because obviously an arrangement for a high, narrow shelf will be different from one intended to stand on a low chest, or in the centre of the dining table.

2 Choose the type of arrangement you are to make.

3 Choose a style.

4 Choose a variation. This will become easier and easier as you come to memorize the different styles and variations; one glance at a branch will be enough for you to know immediately the style and variation in which its beauty will show to the best effect.

5 Choose a container with care, it will be an integral part of the arrangement. Its colour should suit the plant material, the surface on which it is to stand, the background, the light and the season.

6 Choose the plant material. Remember that in all the basic styles and their variations the dictates of nature must be strictly observed. Natural materials grow and reach towards the sun, so that, when making an arrangement, in the position in which it will be placed, you should imagine that you are the sun, and place your plant material accordingly. Incidentally, arrangements to be viewed from four sides are made as if there were four suns.

# Chapter Four

# Risshin Kei

In the Sogetsu School the student is first taught the Risshin Kei, or Upright Style, in which the placing of the main branches is governed by a simple rule. If you understand and memorize this rule before starting on your first arrangement, you will have no difficulty in mastering the basic style and its different variations.

All you need to remember is that, in the Upright Style, Shin, the longest branch, is always in the upright position, with its tip at $5°-15°$ from the imaginary zero line which rises vertically from the centre of the kenzan or pinholder. It may change its position but not its angle.

Soe, the secondary branch, and Hikae, the tertiary, however, are interchangeable in both position and angle, the latter being $45°$ and $75°$ respectively. This means that Soe, for instance, can be at an angle of $45°$, occupying one of several possible positions on the kenzan in relation to the Shin. In this case the Hikae will invariably be at an angle of $75°$. If, on the other hand, the angle of Soe is $75°$, that of Hikae must be $45°$.

The position of the kenzan in the container depends on the lines of the arrangement. For your guidance, suggestions are given in each case. To refresh your memory on the six positions of the kenzan, please refer to the corresponding diagram.

In Upright Style arrangements the jushi can be branches, leaves or flowers. Their positioning gives full scope to your eye and artistic gifts. If you study the suggestions below, you will soon be able to indulge your own creative talents.

Always consult the elevation diagrams for the angles of the main lines, and the bird's-eye plans for their positions.

For our first arrangement, the Basic Upright, we shall use branches for all three main lines, and flowers and branches for the jushi. First study your branches to identify their positive and negative sides, as these will decide the position for which they are most suitable, and also whether your arrangement will incline to the left or to the right.

The positive side of a branch, called Yo in Japanese,

is the one which grows facing the sun; the negative side, called In, is the one facing the dark earth. They are also called male and female, or sunlight and shadow sides. You must use careful discrimination to bring the positive and negative aspects into proportion, since this is one of the secrets of good flower arranging. An arrangement showing positive sides only would lack contrast. Besides, in Ikebana arrangements our aim is to reproduce the universe, which is based on the sound balance of positive and negative factors; so it is only common sense to emulate this balance in our work.

When considering the possibilities of your branches, bear in mind that in a left-hand arrangement movement is to the left, and in a right-hand one it is to the right; and that in the Basic Upright Style the Soe line always follows and supports Shin. This means that, when selecting plant material for this arrangement, you must find two branches which curve in the same direction. You must also trim broken and diseased leaves.

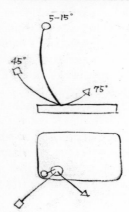

Let us start with a right-hand Basic Upright arrangement, kenzan position 1 or 4. Select your Shin and measure it by the size of the container, as explained in Chapter Three. Cut the base of the branch at an angle and split it. This will enable the pins of the kenzan to pierce and hold it securely. Holding the branch firmly in both hands, put it on the centre back of the kenzan, press it on the pins in an upright position, and then, pressing hard at its base with your fingers, bend it carefully to the desired angle of 5°–15° from the imaginary zero line, and so that it points towards your left shoulder. The branch should be so firmly driven on to the pinholder that when you lift it, the pinholder rises with it.

Now measure the Soe branch according to the Shin; cut it to the required length, which is three-quarters of the latter, and put it on the left front of the pinholder. Once again, do this in the upright position and then bend the branch so that its tip will be at 45° from the imaginary zero line, and coming towards your left shoulder.

Hikae, measured by Soe, is then placed at the right front of the pinholder, opposite Soe, and made to rise at an angle of 75°, and towards your right shoulder.

There are now three branches on your kenzan, all three coming forward. Their bases form a triangle whose apex is at the back. Now is the moment to do your second trimming. Take a good look at the branches. You have created a good deal of space between Shin and Hikae, but there may be too many leaves and laterals on Shin and Soe, interfering with the purity and elegance of the lines. Cut away all overlapping leaves and crossing side-shoots. If the main lines have particularly beautiful curves, you may emphasize these by trimming all the leaves from one side. But giving this extra emphasis needs practice and experience. Think hard before removing apparently superfluous elements; once they are off, you cannot put them back again.

The seasons have much bearing on the amount of trimming we do at this stage. Bare branches are clearly more appropriate in winter, while in summer, an opulent season, we remove fewer leaves from the branches.

Having completed the trimming, look again at your three main branches. In this arrangement the space known as the Pool of Thought is between Shin and Hikae. This is a very important part of your arrangement which must be strictly respected. The masters stress the great importance, in any arrangement, of line and space. You must therefore decide which of the main lines you wish to emphasize by leaving it "lonely". In this arrangement we shall choose Soe. You must also consider the Pool of Thought at the very first placing of your branches. If your stems look untidy at the base and you want to camouflage them by adding a few leaves, make sure that these, or any other components, for that matter, do not protrude into the Pool of Thought.

Now let us add the jushi. The following suggestions are only meant to give the beginner a start in the right direction, until experience and a rapidly developing visual sense provide suitable alternatives. In this arrangement the first jushi supports the Hikae branch. Remember that it can be up to two-thirds of the length of the branch it supports. Add a shorter second jushi to support the first one. Next, add a third jushi to support the upright Shin, and a

fourth one to act as a shadow to Shin. This being a right-hand arrangement, the fourth jushi will occupy a ten-o'clock position.

In Ikebana terminology a main branch, though "lonely", should not be isolated, so that in fact you may find that a fifth jushi is necessary to support the base of Soe.

There is no firm rule governing the number of jushi that can be added. We are taught that as there is no symmetry in nature, we should not strive for symmetry in our arrangements, either. Using an even number of flowers may easily result in a symmetrical effect. But if there is symmetry, there is perfect balance. If there is perfect balance, there is no movement. If there is no movement, the arrangement is lifeless, and you do not want your arrangement to

*Upright Style, Basic*
*Iris with branches of Salix daphnoides*

appear dead. Therefore in the early stages it is advisable to use an uneven number of jushi. Having an even number is not incorrect, provided the result does not look too rigidly balanced.

Complete your arrangement by placing a few short jushi of your branch material in the centre. Arrangers often tend to use branches for their main lines and flowers for their jushi, but this does not create a sense of unity; some material of the main lines must be introduced as jushi.

Before going on, practise placing the main lines with several different materials and combine them in various ways. Use branches for both main lines and jushi; take flowers for the main lines and leaves for the jushi; or choose a group of slender branches for Shin, another group for Soe, and leaves or flowers for Hikae. But whatever the combination, you need judicious trimming to emphasize the particular beauty of your material, whether it lies in the bark, in the line or in the leaves.

The Basic Upright is one of the most popular fundamental styles; it can be used for creating big arrangements. Most of the early Ikebana arrangements were designed to stand in the tokonoma, the ceremonial alcove of the traditional Japanese room, which meant that they were seen from the front only. But in Western homes there is no tokonoma, and our arrangements normally stand on a low side table or a chest in the hall, where they can be viewed from at least two sides. The jushi we have added as a "shadow" to Shin gives enough additional depth to provide another visual aspect, and so this Basic Upright Style can be viewed from two sides.

*Variation No. 1*

This is an open arrangement which looks particularly attractive on a deep sideboard or a corner table. The elegance of its line depends very much on the correct positioning of the kenzan, which, for this variation, differs from the general rule. For a left-hand arrangement it goes into position No. 1, in the left front corner of the container. For a right-hand one use position No. 2. Only these two front positions can be used because the backward-leaning Shin branch is using a section of the back of the horizontal circle around the zero line.

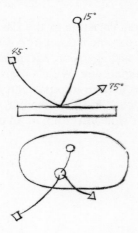

For a left-hand arrangement place Shin on the centre back of the kenzan, going back diagonally to the right-hand corner at an angle of 15°. Soe is placed on the kenzan at the left front and comes forward at 45°, towards your left shoulder. This, forms a continuous line from the tip of Shin right down to the heart of the arrangement, and up to the tip of Soe, which is why this is called an open arrangement. Hikae stands at the right front of the kenzan and crosses the front of the container towards your right shoulder, at 75°.

In this variation the backward line of Shin is balanced by the expanse of water behind it. The Pool of Thought will be between Shin and Soe. Keep your jushi low and in the centre to emphasize the openness of the arrangement.

*Variation No. 2*

This arrangement is perfect for displaying an arched flowering branch to be viewed from above. Place it on a low coffee table to get the best effect. It is also good for grouping lines, by using several gracefully curved stems of willow, dogwood or spiraea for each main line.

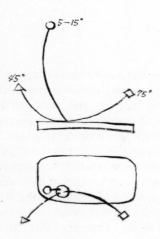

The kenzan is placed to allow the Soe line to cross the front of the container at about three-quarters of the distance between the kenzan and the far side of the container. This means that for a right-hand arrangement your kenzan position is No. 1 or No. 4. Soe, placed on the right front of the kenzan at 75°, crosses the right front of the container, pointing beyond your right shoulder. This gives the arrangement great elegance. Shin stands at the centre back of the kenzan, inclined at an angle of 15°, to the left side. Hikae is placed at the left front, opposite Soe, inclining to the left front at 45° and, in fact, supporting Shin.

If using flowering branches you may find that Shin needs the support of a long jushi. Hikae would also be supported by jushi, Soe being left as the "lonely one". The Pool of Thought is between Shin and Soe.

*Variation No. 3*

This arrangement is designed to be viewed from three sides. The kenzan can occupy any one of the six positions. I suggest that we place it at the centre back of the container, in position No. 6, to give greater depth, or at the centre front, in position No. 5, if we want a flat effect.

If you look at the bird's-eye view plan, you can see that Shin and Soe open like a fan. Shin, at 15°, is at the left back of the kenzan, inclining slightly towards your left shoulder. Soe, opposite Shin, is bending in the opposite direction towards your right shoulder, at an angle of 45°. Hikae is at the centre front, at 75°.

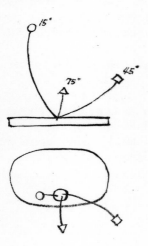

Hikae being by far the most difficult line to place in this arrangement, sometimes it is put into position first. The jushi will be fairly low, concentrated on Hikae and Soe. In this right-hand arrangement the shadow jushi is in the ten-o'clock position. The Pool of Thought is between Shin and Soe, at the back. This is perhaps why nine times out of ten you use position No. 5 for the kenzan, which allows you to emphasize the space at the back of the container. This arrangement fits in particularly well with a Western décor. It looks especially beautiful when flowers are used for both main lines and jushi. Try it with tulips, roses, stocks, chrysanthemums or poppies.

As this variation is for viewing from three sides, you cannot consider it finished unless you turn your container around to make sure that the kenzan does not look unsightly from a viewing position of about three feet to the left, right and centre front. If there is an unattractive aspect, use small leaves, or, if you have used branches for your main lines, some of the laterals you have trimmed off, to complete it.

## Variation No. 4

This is an Omission Arrangement, sometimes called the Arrangement of Humility, because it is the only one which leaves out Soe, the line representing Man. Unlike Shin and Hikae which stand for Heaven and Earth, Man can occasionally be omitted from the Ikebana representation of the universe.

The Omission Arrangement is most suitable for a corner position. It consists of Shin, Hikae and jushi. The measurement for Hikae is the same as if Soe were used. This variation is a particularly elegant way to display a specimen flower by using a branch for Shin and a lovely camellia or a perfect rose for Hikae. The final effect is that of subtle simplicity, but, like all truly simple and beautiful creations, this

*Variation No. 4   Tree peony with bare branches*

arrangement takes a little extra patience and effort. In our diagram for a right-hand arrangement Shin stands at the centre back of the pinholder, and Hikae at the right front, as in the Basic Upright Style. Indeed, any of the earlier variations can be made in the Omission Style by following the instructions but leaving out the Soe line altogether. The position of the kenzan naturally depends on the variation you choose.

To make the Omission Variation of the Basic Upright, you should put the kenzan in position No. 1 or 4 for a right-hand arrangement, and position No. 2 or 3 for a left-hand one. We choose a right-hand one, putting the kenzan into position No. 4. Shin is at the centre back of the pinholder, with its tip coming to the left side and front, at an angle of

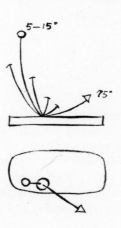

*Upright Style, Variation No. 1    Strelitzia reginae in circular container.
The kenzan is camouflaged with driftwood and pebbles*

15°. Hikae is on the right front of the kenzan, inclining towards your right shoulder, at an angle of 75°.

If you wish to give the Shin line a long jushi, place this supporter behind it. Putting it in front of Shin you might easily form the usual triangle with the tips of the components, which would defeat the purpose of the Omission Style.

If you use branches for both Shin and Hikae, remember to concentrate your jushi on the Hikae line. This will add weight at the base and thus balance the long branch which is in the Upright Position.

*Variation No. 2   Bare viburnum branch with orange tulips suggests the idea of winter turning into spring. Modern stoneware container*

*Variation No. 5   Weeping willow with irises*

### Variation No. 5

This is a Divided Arrangement – in Japanese, kabuwaki, which means to divide or share. It allows us to carry out any of the previous variations by taking away one main line from the other two and putting it on a separate kenzan at the back, to the front, or to one side of the container. The choice of positions is yours, so long as you do not put the two groups level with each other. If one is to the front, the other one should be to the back.

The sun-and-moon kenzan, which locks into one piece but can be divided, is ideal for this variation.

If, in the spirit of Ikebana, you pay close attention to the seasons, in winter you will tend to place the main group to the front in order to obscure much of the water in the low container which might otherwise look chilling. But in summer the correct place for the main group is at the back so that more of the cool water can be seen.

You may, of course, put your large group at the back even in winter, but restore the seasonal balance by bringing the small group nearer to the large one, thus covering up a large expanse of water.

*Variation No. 3 combines Salix daphnoides with amaryllis in circular ceramic dish*

*Opposite page Variation No. 3*
*Pink feathers in iced glass Iwata container*

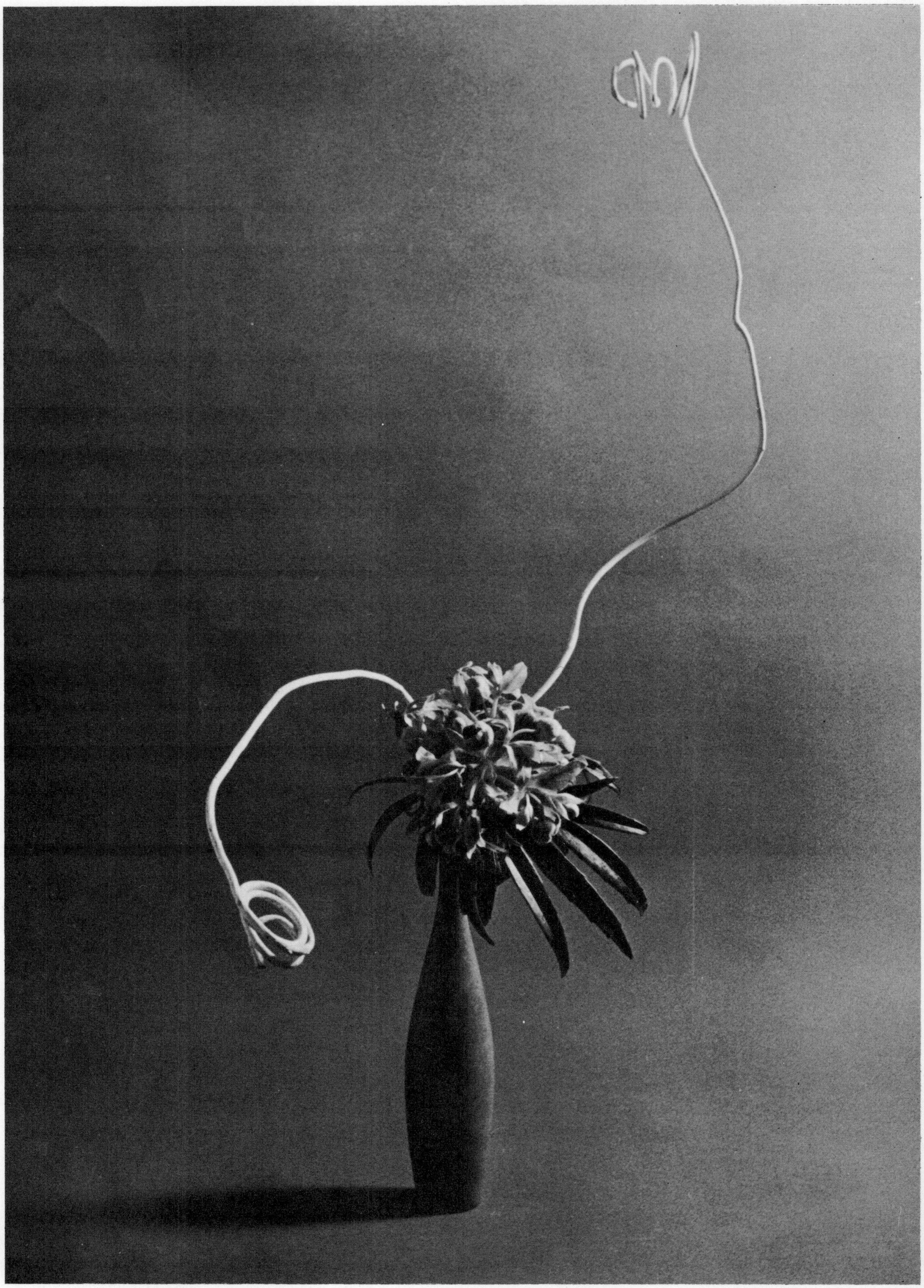

Let us make a right-handed Divided Arrangement of Variation No. 2. The main kenzan with Shin and Hikae is placed at the left front of the container. The second kenzan, holding Soe, stands at the back of the container.

Soe crosses towards your right shoulder, at 75°, supported by a jushi which is bending low over the pinholder. Shin is at the back of the main kenzan, standing slightly to the side towards your left shoulder, at an angle of 15°. Hikae is on the left front of the same kenzan, coming directly towards your left shoulder, at an angle of 45°.

The jushi in the main group support both Shin and Hikae.

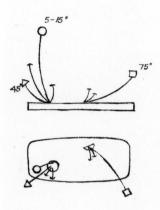

This is a particularly beautiful arrangement to make in the summer. As you can see from the bird's-eye view, the Soe line comes right across the water and is reflected in it. The angles of the branches and the distance between the two kenzans put a strong accent on space. Because of its divided nature, this arrangement has no Pool of Thought.

*Variation No. 6*

As this arrangement is to be viewed from four sides, the kenzan is placed off centre in a circular container. First we divide the horizontal circle around the imaginary zero line into three equal arcs and place our branches accordingly. Shin, which in this variation is normally measured by the standard size, stands at the left front of the kenzan, with its tip at 15° from the zero line, pointing at your left shoulder. Soe is at the right front of the kenzan, rising to an angle of 45°, and Hikae is at the centre back of the kenzan, at 75°.

The first jushi plays the role of a supporter to Soe. It is half the length of Soe and lies almost directly beneath it. The second jushi is about half the length of Hikae and stands between Shin and Hikae. Shin, being in the upright position, has no supporter behind it, but we place a third jushi in the centre of the container so that it rises slightly towards Shin. Now turn the arrangement round and add jushi wherever necessary. Their placing depends on where the finished arrangement is to stand. Remember that it must look attractive from all sides.

This arrangement has no Pool of Thought. The purity of the main lines is vitally important, and the space between the top half of them should be left clear.

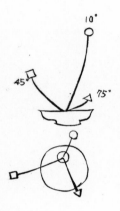

*Opposite page Variation No. 4*
*Dried vine is used for Shin and Hikae,*
*Helleborus viridis for jushi, in bronze*
*bottle container*

*Classical arrangement of chrysanthemums*

*Basic Keishin Kei arrangement using
flowering peach branches only in rectangular black container*

# Chapter Five

# Keishin Kei

Arrangements in Keishin Kei, of the Slanting Style, are based on the angles of 15°, 45°, and 75°. Although these may sound familiar from the instructions for Risshin Kei, the Upright Style, the two groups are very different.

In all Keishin Kei arrangements the tip of the Shin branch is always at an angle of 45° from the imaginary zero line which rises vertically from the centre of the kenzan. It is this 45° angle of the most important branch that gives these arrangements their slanting character.

The Shin line in Keishin Kei never changes its angle, only its position. On the other hand the Soe and Hikae lines may interchange both their angles – of 15° and 75° respectively – and their positions.

Keishin Kei arrangements look their best and give the greatest visual pleasure when made with branches which grow in planes, e.g. the beech, mountain ash, azalea and some kinds of viburnum. Flowers with long, bare stems, such as gerberas and poppies, also look most effective in this style.

The low 45° angle of Shin, the Heaven branch, expresses the ancient truth that Heaven is all around and not simply above us. But Man should always look to Heaven. Hence, although in Keishin Kei arrangements Soe, the Man line, may be higher than Shin, its tip must always incline and look towards the latter.

As a rule, for all slanting arrangements Shin is cut to the small or the standard measurement.

Let us start with the basic Keishin Kei which is most suitable for displaying flowering branches on a low table. It accentuates the beauty of spring flowering branches – almond, peach or plum – which are seldom used after their flowering period has ended. Personally I prefer to use these branches by themselves; I feel there is no need to supplement them with other spring flowers.

The kenzan position is No. 2 or No. 3 for arrangements that sweep to the left, and No. 1 or No. 4 for those sweeping to the right. As in all basic styles, every line in this arrangement comes forward. Whether you make a left- or right-hand arrangement

depends on the positive or negative aspect of your branches.

Let us place the kenzan in position No. 3. Shin will stand at its left front, crossing the container diagonally towards your left shoulder at an angle of 45° from the vertical. Soe is placed at the centre back of the kenzan at 15°, following the Shin line towards your left shoulder. Hikae is placed at the right front of the kenzan, opposite Shin, and crosses diagonally to the right of your right shoulder, at an angle of 75°. In this arrangement the jushi may be low and central. Shin, as the "lonely one", is then supported at the base by a short jushi which will accentuate its loneliness. The Pool of Thought is between Soe and Hikae.

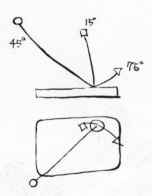

As an alternative, use branches for Shin and Soe, and flowers for Hikae; or branches for Shin and Hikae, and flowers for Soe.

Although you are offered alternative positions for the kenzan, you will probably prefer the rear positions for slanting arrangements, because a branch coming forward, at 45°, gains better balance from the expanse of water in front of it, especially when Soe also is leaning to the front.

In Keishin Kei we are encouraged to put small pieces of root or pebbles in the water to cover the kenzan and for additional interest. In some arrangements a suitable root can even take the role of Hikae, supported by jushi of flowers and branches.

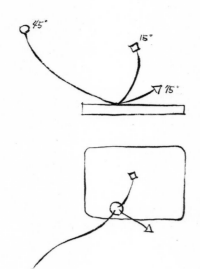

Just as in Risshin Kei, the first variation of Keishin Kei has a special rule for placing the kenzan. For an arrangement sweeping to the left, it will be placed at the left of the container, and vice versa.

Let us make a left-hand arrangement, with the kenzan in position No. 1. The Shin line is placed at the left front of the kenzan, coming forward, at an angle of $45°$, pointing slightly left of your left shoulder. Soe at the centre back continues the diagonal, to the rear, at $15°$. Hikae stands opposite Shin at the right front of the kenzan, coming diagonally towards your right shoulder, at $75°$. This variation is often made as a "welcome" arrangement, using the branches of the willow, birch, or of any other tree which has tiny leaves, so that the

*Slanting Style, Variation No. 1    Yellow Arum lilies and Griselinia littoralis in a rectangular white container with green inside*

*Arrangement of Fatsia japonica and Australian Protea,*
*in salt-glaze stoneware container made by the author*

light tip of Shin will move gently in the breeze when a door or window is opened. This is yet another example of the subtle symbolism of Ikebana; in Japan the fluttering of the hand is a gesture of welcome, and the slight movement of the tip of the Shin branch in this variation imitates that gesture. If you choose a heavy branch – rhododendron for example – for your Shin branch, the position of the kenzan could be No. 3 for a left-hand arrangement. Placed in position No. 1, the main branch would look too heavy coming over the edge of the container. This, however, is an exception. Generally speaking, the chief characteristic of this variation is openness, as the second main branch goes to the rear of the imaginary zero line, continuing the line of Shin, and is balanced by the expanse of container behind it.

To stress this air of spaciousness, place short jushi to Shin. Soe is supported at the base in the front, with the shadow jushi in the two-o'clock position. Hikae is left as the "lonely one". The Pool of Thought is between Shin and Soe.

*Variation No. 2*

This variation, with its two long main lines coming forward at low angles, is particularly suitable for a high shelf or wall container. It also makes a beautiful Nageire arrangement in a tall container, the technique of which will be described in a following chapter. You have a choice of kenzan positions No. 1, 2, 3 or 4; 2 or 3 for arrangements flowing to the left, 1 or 4 for those to the right. More often than not, one would use the rear positions for depth.

For a right-hand arrangement, place the kenzan in position No. 4. Shin will stand at the right front of the kenzan at $45°$, coming towards your right shoulder. Soe, opposite Shin on the left front of the kenzan, comes towards your left shoulder, at $75°$. As both are low, but for the difference in their length they would form a perfect fan when viewed from above.

Hikae, placed at the centre back of the kenzan, follows the Shin line, at $15°$.

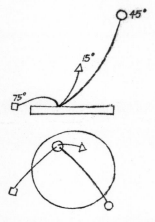

All variations will assume different expressions according to the placing of the jushi. Here we support Shin and Hikae, and, if the Soe branch is heavily

leaved, give it no jushi. Alternatively if your Soe is a branch which grows in planes or bends gracefully by nature, give it a supporter for about one-third of its length only.

In this variation the Pool of Thought is between Soe and Hikae.

It is worth bearing in mind that there is a far greater difference between No. 2 Slanting and No. 2 Upright than between any other "twin" variations. Don't be lulled into false security by thinking that you can make a No. 2 Keishin Kei arrangement simply by exchanging the Shin and Hikae of the No. 2 Risshin Kei.

*Variation No. 3*

This arrangement is designed to be viewed from three sides. In principle the kenzan can be placed in any of the six regular positions, but as this arrangement is distinctly asymmetrical, with Hikae rising from the centre front, position No. 6 is, I think, the most suitable, especially for beginners. Its main advantage is that it leaves plenty of space in the container for the placing of Hikae.

For a right-hand version, Shin is at the left rear of the kenzan, coming forward, towards your left shoulder, at an angle of $45°$. Soe stands at the right rear opposite Shin, coming slightly forward towards your right shoulder, at $15°$. Hikae forms the apex of the triangle at the centre front, coming directly towards you, at $75°$.

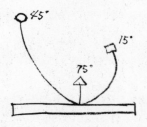

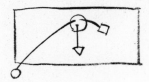

This variation looks attractive in a low position. I myself prefer it at normal table height. In the latter case the jushi may be compact, supporting Soe and Hikae and leaving Shin as "the lonely one". To add depth, place the shadow jushi behind Soe in the two-o'clock position. The Pool of Thought is at the back, between Shin and Soe.

*Variation No. 4*

We can base this Omission Style on any of the previous variations, or on the fundamental basic style, using Shin and Hikae and omitting Soe, the Man line. In symbolical terms this variation will be in praise of humility. Choose whichever variation you please, but consider where your arrangement is to stand, and observe the dictates of the branches or flowers you wish to use.

Let us choose Variation No. 2, inclining to the right. We shall use a light branch of gypsophila for Shin and a flower for Hikae. The kenzan is placed in position No. 1 or 4, at the left of the container.

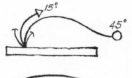

Place Shin on the right front of the kenzan so that it comes towards your right shoulder at an angle of 45°. Hikae, at 15°, follows the line of Shin from the centre back of the kenzan.

Choose a Shin with delicate tracery, so that Hikae can shelter behind it, creating an impression of charming modesty.

*Variation No. 5*

This is a Divided Arrangement which is made by taking one main line from a complete arrangement and placing it on a separate kenzan. Of course you must make every effort to safeguard the character of the original arrangement. Any of the previous variations may be divided in this way.

The positions of the two kenzans will depend on the

*Variation No. 3   Flowering cherry with lily-flowered Aladdin tulips in kidney-shaped Moribana container*

season of the year, on your material, and on the variation you have chosen. Two containers may be used.

Whatever you do, remember that in this variation the aim is to create a natural scene. Do not allow your branches to touch the side of the container or the pieces of wood or rock you may place in front of the kenzan. This rule applies to all Moribana arrangements.

Let us make a Divided Arrangement of Variation No. 1 of Keishin Kei. Because of the open character of this variation, we use the small measurement for Shin, which equals the diameter plus the depth of the container. The other branches are measured in proportion to this.

For a left-hand "summer" arrangement which means

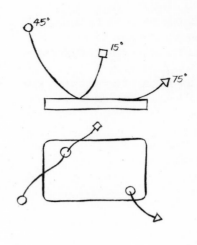

*Variation No. 4  Camellia branches and jonquils in a salt-glaze stoneware container*

showing an expanse of water, place the main kenzan in position No. 4, in the left rear corner of the container, and the secondary one in position No. 2, in the right front corner.

Shin is placed on the left front of the main kenzan, going out of the container towards your left shoulder, at 45°. Soe goes from the centre back of the kenzan to the rear of the imaginary horizontal circle around the zero line, at an angle of 15°, forming a continuation of Shin.

Place Hikae on the second kenzan so that it crosses the edge of the container towards your right shoulder, at 75°.

Arrange the jushi around the base of Shin, Soe, and Hikae, keeping them less compact than in other variations. As we have plenty of space between

kenzans and branches, there is no specific Pool of Thought. Placed in a large container, this Divided Arrangement will look cool and spacious.

Try it with flowering branches for the main lines and small ferns for the jushi. Tulips with primroses, and monstera leaves with hyacinths also give a charming effect.

You may place a "bridge" of driftwood between the two kenzans, but do not let it connect them; this would create too strong a link, and dispel the idea of division. It is better to suggest no more than a subtle link by placing one end of the wood in front of one kenzan, and the other to the rear of the second.

*Variation No. 5 In two matching triangular containers. Carnations with Ligustrum ovalifolium, the garden privet*

*Variation No. 6*

This is especially suitable for a large exhibition piece which is to stand on the floor of a long hall. Soe and Hikae are duplicated and divide the circle around the zero line equally with the Shin line. The second Soe branch is almost below the first one, and is slightly shorter. This also applies to Hikae. Shin, Soe, and Hikae are at the angles of 45°, 75° and 15° respectively.

Your Shin line could be a heavy but shapely root, with branches or flowers for Soe and Hikae. The jushi could be smaller roots, clumps of flowers, or tight bunches of evergreens. Another suggestion is to use a large dead branch for Shin, a large root for Soe, and a mass of green foliage and self-coloured flowers for Hikae.

If you decide to use roots or dead branches, take care not to make the arrangement too solid. Create points of balance so that there is plenty of light and space between the base of the roots and the board or floor on which the arrangement is placed if no container is used. But do not go to the other extreme by combining one heavy root with light materials; proper balance must be achieved.

A simple Variation No. 6 can be made with Iceland Poppies or asters for both main lines and jushi. Place the kenzan off centre in a large container, and in the centre of a small one. An asymmetrical look can be achieved by using an off-centre section of the kenzan as well as by placing the kenzan itself off centre. It must be borne in mind that this arrangement is intended to be viewed from all four sides.

# Chapter Six

# Haishin Kei

Strictly speaking Haishin Kei, the Flat Style, belongs to the Slanting Style, as does Suishin Kei, the Hanging Style. But for the sake of clarity I prefer to introduce them in separate chapters. (Suishin Kei is discussed in Chapter Seven.)

It is the characteristic of the Flat Style that the angle of Shin remains constant at 75°–85°, although its position can change. Soe and Hikae, however, can not only interchange their position – they did so in the previous styles, too – but their angles are not constant either, so that you must learn a slightly different formula for each variation.

Let me make this point clear. In both Risshin Kei and Keishin Kei the angles are always 75°, 45° and 15°, however variously they may be distributed among the main lines. But in Haishin Kei the angles may be 60°, 85° and 75°, or 15°, 85° and 35°, or even 85°, 35° and 110°, depending on the variation. It is because of this peculiarity that Haishin Kei is not taught in the Sogetsu School until the arranger is a fairly advanced student who has achieved mastery over the less variable Upright and Slanting Styles. The low position of Shin makes Haishin Kei arrangements ideal for viewing from above. Indeed, one would rarely place one at a height exceeding 4 ft.; it truly comes into its own as a table arrangement. In most Haishin Kei arrangements the small or the standard measurement is used for Shin.

In the basic Haishin Kei, as in all other basic fundamental styles, the tips of all three main lines come forward. Let us make this as a left-hand arrangement, with the kenzan in position No. 2 or 3. The space between the kenzan and the edge of the container must be at least the thickness of a finger. Shin is placed on the left front of the kenzan, crossing diagonally to your left shoulder, at an angle of 85°. Soe, standing at the centre back, follows behind Shin at 45°. Hikae is placed at the right front of the kenzan, opposite Shin, crossing diagonally towards your right shoulder at, 75°.

This highly adaptable arrangement looks most attractive with branches for Shin and Hikae, and flowers for Soe; jushi will then support Soe and Shin, and Hikae remains the "lonely one", with only a supporter at its base. The shadow jushi will be at the back of Soe, at about ten o'clock. The Pool of Thought is between Soe and Hikae.

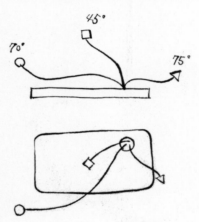

Red turkey oak for Shin and Hikae with rust-coloured chrysanthemums for Soe makes a gorgeous autumn arrangement in this style.

*Variation No. 1*

This arrangement has a flat and forward-moving effect and is particularly suitable for a narrow cabinet or shelf. If you want it to sweep to the right, place your kenzan in position No. 4, to the left rear of the container.

Shin stands at the right front of the kenzan, coming towards your right shoulder, at an angle of 85°. One word of warning, though. The edge of the container being at 90°, make sure that Shin, bending low at 85°, does not touch it, not even to the extent of a leaf resting on the edge, as this would give the arrangement an air of heaviness.

Soe is at the centre back of the kenzan, at 10°, going diagonally to the rear and continuing the line of Shin. Hikae is on the left front of the kenzan, moving across the edge of the container, at 75°.

The Pool of Thought is between Shin and Soe. Jushi go to Shin and Soe. Hikae is the "lonely one".

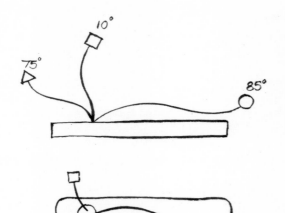

As an alternative, try this variation with branches for Shin and Soe, flowers for Hikae. A particularly attractive version has smilax fern for Shin and Soe and pastel antirrhinums for Hikae, with a mixture of the two as supporters.

When placing the jushi, take care not to give too much upright emphasis to this or any other flat arrangement.

*Variation No. 2*

With long branches and low jushi, this variation can be made as a wind-swept arrangement, or, with driftwood and branches, as a water-view one.

To make a left-hand water-view arrangement, place the kenzan in position No. 2 or 3. Let us choose No. 3 this time. Shin goes on the centre back of the

*Basic Haishin Kei arrangement. Salix glandulosa setsuka and double cream-coloured freesias symbolizing moonlight, in a black stoneware container*

kenzan and flows across the water almost horizontally, at 75°. Use a curly piece of wood or a gnarled root for Soe. Place this at the left front of the kenzan, at 85°, to run slightly to the front of Shin. Hikae, on the right front of the kenzan, flows to the left at 35°, covering the bases of Shin and Soe.

The choice of your jushi will depend on how much foliage there is on the Shin and Hikae branches. They should cover the base of Soe and support Hikae. This variation being particularly suitable for a spring arrangement, use young branches in leaf, bud or blossom for the main lines, and tulips or ranunculus for jushi. In summer use copper beech branches and the beautiful blue-pink Prelude rose for jushi.

Impaling a piece of wood or root on the kenzan is

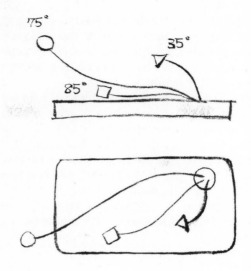

*Variation No. 1    Flat Style arrangement of Chaenomeles japonica maulei with peony-flowered double tulips, in a Japanese basket*

difficult and bad for the pin-holder. I suggest that you hold your branch or root at the angle it is to be placed at and make a horizontal mark in pencil or chalk where the flat base is to be. Saw along this line with your handsaw.

With a hammer and some slender nails fix a piece of thin, flat boxwood to the base of your branch or root, so that it juts out to the right for a couple of inches. Now place the branch or root in the container and put the kenzan on the protruding piece of boxwood. The weight of the kenzan will keep your branch or root in position.

If the inside of the container is dark, cover the auxiliary piece of boxwood with non-toxic dark paint.

*Variation No. 3*

This is an excellent arrangement to place on a high shelf or wall bracket, as its three lines flow to the left, the right and the front respectively.

If you wish to make a left-hand arrangement, place your kenzan to the centre-front of the container.

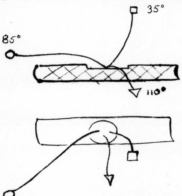

Shin will flow from the left rear of the kenzan at an angle of 85°, towards your left shoulder. Soe, placed opposite Shin, goes towards your right shoulder at 35°. Hikae flows from the centre front of the kenzan to the front, its tip ending below the lip of the container, at an angle of 110°. As Hikae is the most difficult line to place in this arrangement, it is often put in position first.

This variation is eminently suitable for Nageire, as described in Chapter Seven.

*Variation No. 4*

This Omission Style can be based on any of the earlier Haishin Kei variations. But as the Shin is at a very low angle in all of them, we tend to make this variation in bottles and moon-shaped containers as explained in the chapters on Nageire and on classical arrangements. Shin is usually cut to the small measurement length.

Let us make an Omission Style arrangement from Variation No. 1, in a Moribana container. For a left-hand arrangement the kenzan is in position No. 3. Shin, at the left front of your kenzan, goes towards your left shoulder, at an angle of 85°. Hikae crosses the front of the container, at 75°, towards

your right shoulder. Jushi are added to support Shin and mass at the base of Hikae.

Use dried vine for the main lines, or carefully dried and twisted prunings from the wistaria, and flowers for the jushi.

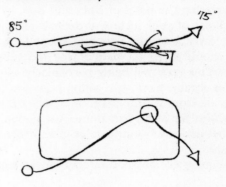

*Variation No. 5*

This popular Divided Arrangement has a flat, compact effect. It is made on two kenzans which you may put in one or two containers. If you use two separate containers, place them diagonally opposite each other either on a table or close together on a base.

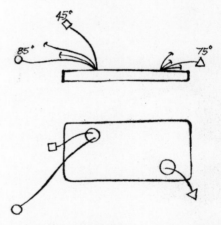

Let us make a Divided Arrangement of the basic Haishin Kei, placing two kenzans diagonally opposite each other in one container. The first kenzan in position No. 4 will hold Shin and Soe, the second one in position No. 2 will contain Hikae.

Shin, at the left front of the kenzan, crosses the edge of the container towards your left shoulder, at an angle of 85°. Soe follows the Shin line from the centre back of the kenzan at 45°. Hikae, on the second kenzan, crosses the edge towards your right shoulder at an angle of 75°, looking back towards the tip of Shin.

Support Shin with jushi on the right. Leave Soe as the "lonely one". On the second kenzan jushi will follow the line of Hikae, their leaves shading its base. No part of either kenzan should be visible

*Opposite page*
*Gerbera and asparagus plumosus fern in pale green antique glass bottle*

*Combination of Variations Nos. 5 and 6*
*Pink Carol roses are used for both*
*main lines and jushi, in two*
*blue-green salt-glaze stoneware*
*containers by Rosemary Wren*

from the normal viewing distance of 3 ft.
This variation looks enchanting in tiny Carol or
Garnet roses.

*Variation No. 6*

Being flat, most Haishin Kei variations make first-
class table arrangements, and Variation No. 6 is a
natural choice for the dinner table.
Make it in a circular container, or on a tray using
a well kenzan. Shin should measure the diameter
of the container only. A long Shin, going far beyond
the edge of the container, would be a nuisance to
your guests. Besides, the passing of dishes could
dislodge flowers and reduce the arrangement to an
untidy mess.
Place the kenzan to one side of the circular container,
at a finger's breadth from the inside wall. Give Shin
the appearance of extra length by putting it on the
inside edge of the kenzan, i.e. the one nearest to the
centre of the container. Let it cross the container at
its widest expanse, at an angle of 85°.
Soe, rising at 45°, forms a sector of about one-third
of a circle with Shin. Hikae, at 75°, forms an identical
sector on the other side of Shin, crossing the container
at its narrowest part. In fact your three main
branches divide the imaginary circle around the
kenzan into three equal arcs, with Soe making the
highest point.

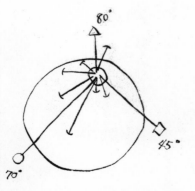

The jushi should be kept low, and in the centre.
Their placing needs special care if the arrangement

is not to look heavy. The finished version must look
equally attractive from all sides, giving each guest
a pleasing view.
You may find the following pattern helpful in placing
the jushi. Take the first one, which should measure
half the length of Shin, and place it between Shin
and Soe, but supporting Shin. Put the next one to
support Soe, standing between Soe and Hikae, and
the third one to Hikae, keeping it so short that it just
clears the water, standing between Hikae and Shin.
The fourth jushi, chosen for the perfection of its
shape or colour, goes in the centre of the kenzan,
slightly inclining towards Shin.
As you place further jushi, turn the container around
to check that neither the kenzan nor some ugly stem
is showing, or that, conversely, a beautiful stem or
leaf is not obscured. Use flowers, branches or leaves
for jushi, but do not pack your material too tightly.
Remember, space can be one of the most attractive
features.
Mix sweet peas with light ferns in this variation, or
orchids with foliage. Use roses supported by pale
beech or pine. Pine branches supported by roses
also look exquisite. The range of plant material is
almost endless. But do not use heavy flowers on thin
stems as main branches. Carnations, for instance,
make excellent jushi but poor main lines.
Another version of Variation No. 6 has a cool quality
which makes it a refreshing choice for a hot day.
Use an oval "lake" container, placing the kenzan just
off centre at the narrow end, in position No. 2 or 3.
If position No. 3 is used, Shin at 85° stands at the
centre-back of the kenzan, crossing the long edge of
the container on its own side. Soe stands at the left
front of the kenzan at an angle of 60°, crossing the
front of the container. Completing the equal sectors
of the circle, Hikae, at 75°, crosses the narrow end
of the container.
These placings result in a large expanse of cool
water in which one or two petals of the flowers you
have used may float freely. Don't add petals from
other flowers. The jushi should be short and light.
Use flowers to support the base of Shin and Soe.

# Chapter Seven

# Nageire

Nageire means "thrown in", but the term should not be taken literally; no flower arranger, however accomplished, would succeed with so careless a procedure. What we mean by Nageire is a casually elegant arrangement in a neat, tall container, the materials being kept in position without the aid of a kenzan.

This is what makes Nageire basically different from Moribana arrangements which are invariably constructed on one or more kenzans. Although the containers used for the "thrown in" style may range from tall, slender classical vases to oddly shaped, bulbous or asymmetrical vessels, none of them allows the use of a pinholder. But since all Ikebana arrangements require the careful placing of suitably angled components, in Nageire we are taught a variety of fixing methods to make up for the absence of a pinholder. These are known by the term "Kubari".

This in turn means that all the basic arrangements and variations of the Upright, Slanting and Flat Styles can be made in Nageire; furthermore we can also branch out into Suishin Kei, or Hanging Style arrangements which are a speciality of this type. In the Sogetsu School we teach four main fixing methods, all of which use the natural stems of woody plants, with or without the addition of bass or raffia. We do not use wire. Apart from not being a natural material, it is difficult to tie, it rusts, it may mark the container, and the rusting process produces an unpleasant film on the surface of the water. Bass, on the other hand, is an ideal natural material which is easy to tie when dry and tightens when wet. Again, in water its colour grows deeper so that it blends well with the branch it is used on. Last but not least, raffia does not affect the purity of the water, nor will it damage the stem or bark of your plant material.

The woody stems used for fixing arrangements should be fairly supple and straight. Dogwood, willow and pine are ideal for the purpose, but try to avoid branches with a pithy inside because they snap easily. Collect a number of suitable sticks whenever you get the opportunity. Keep them in a little water on your kitchen window-sill; they will last for many weeks.

In every Suishin Kei arrangement it is the size and shape of the container and the bulk and weight of your plant material which determine the type of fixing you will need. Obviously a tall, heavy container, chosen for a big arrangement, requires a strong, thick prop, while a slim, fine glass vase for a delicate arrangement needs only a light support inside.

*Fixing Method No. 1*

In this method the arrangement is held in position by a vertical centre stick inside the container. Ideal for upright styles, it can be used equally well for others.

Cut the stick to make it $\frac{1}{2}$ in. shorter than the inside height of the container, and cut its base straight so that it stands squarely on the base of the vase. With short, straight cuts slice the top end down the centre for about 3 in. Take your time over this; long cuts tend to split the stick rather than cut it, and the split may run off centre; this would greatly diminish the strength of your Kubari.

Now take the Shin branch for the arrangement you have in mind – say Variation No. 1 in the Upright Style – and hold it in your left hand at the angle it is to be placed at in the arrangement. i.e. 15° from the vertical. With your shears in the upright position, cut the base of the Shin branch to make it fit against the inside wall of the container. This procedure is described as keying the position of the branch, and it is a very important step in all Nageire arrangements.

Using once again short, straight cuts, slit the bottom end of the Shin branch vertically to a length which equals at least the diameter of the opening of the container but is not less than 3 in. Interlock this with the slit end of the fixing stick, keeping the latter upright, and rest the keyed end of the Shin branch against the inside wall of the container.

Do this first keying patiently and painstakingly, for in it lies the secret of a successful fixing.

Now choose your Soe branch. If possible, cut it from the base of a branch so that it has an obtuse angle. Key it in the same way as you have done with Shin, remembering that in Variation No. 1, Upright Style, Soe will go diagonally away from Shin, at an angle of 45°. Then split its bottom end and interlock it with either the centre support or the Shin branch, whichever the case may be; make its keyed end rest against the wall of the container opposite the Shin base.

Sometimes it may be necessary to slit the base of Soe horizontally rather than vertically. You can easily judge that for yourself by holding the branch at the correct angle before splitting its end to see how it will best meet and interlock with your prop or your Shin branch.

At this stage you have the ends of two main branches crossed diagonally inside the container, adequately supported and balanced. The balance should be sufficiently firm for the arrangement not to collapse when you carry it from one room to another; it should also remain undisturbed by a breeze.

Your third main branch will be keyed, cut and slit in the same way. Again, you may need a horizontal rather than a vertical slit. Remember that the ends of all three main branches must touch the inner wall of the container, being mutually interlocked with the vertical stick or with each other.

In this, as in all other fixing methods, the jushi are either fitted into the existing fixture of the main branches, or else their stems, cleared of leaves, are left long enough to fit against the wall of the container. In the latter case measure that part of the stem which is to remain above the rim of the container, and twist and bend at this point so that the lower part will rest against the side of the container, and the visible section will be held at the desired angle. The lower the point of contact with the inside of the container, the higher the angle of the jushi.

If you combine branches as main lines with flowers as jushi, bear in mind the unequal life expectation of your plant material. The branches will last for several weeks but the flowers will have to be changed every few days. Do not, therefore, fix the jushi too firmly, otherwise you will be unable to renew them without disturbing the main branches. And the sad fact is that no arrangement can be exactly reconstructed. Even if the supporting stick does not crack, you will not get a wholly satisfactory effect a second time.

There are two important points which apply to all Nageire arrangements. The first one is that the visible space at the base of the stems deserves great attention. In Moribana no part of the plant material is allowed to touch the rim of the container. In Nageire, however, both main branches and jushi may do so. But use this freedom with restraint. Too many stems touching the container would make the arrangement look heavy.

The second important point is to keep the plant material within about one-quarter of the area of the opening of the container. Leaving three-quarters empty allows your materials to breathe, and the water to keep fresh for a longer time. Your arrangement will look better, too. The rising branches and flowers should give an impression of growing together. This can only be achieved by keeping the stems together where they emerge.

Using different quarter sections of the opening enables you to make a greater variety of arrangements, just as in Moribana by using the different positions for the kenzan.

The vertical fixing method will secure the balance of any arrangement so long as the base of the fixing branch rests on the bottom of the container and the ends of the main branches are balanced against an inside wall. If your vertical prop is sturdy enough, it will hold quite a heavy branch firmly in position.

*Fixing No. 2*

This method is based on the use of a crossbar in the shape of the cross of St Andrew. Two slim sticks, roughly of pencil thickness, are placed at right angles to each other and wedged firmly in the neck of the container, about 1 in. below its top edge. It is an excellent method for fixing light foliage arrangements or those of flowers only, and you will find it particularly useful for making cascading arrangements.

Be careful when wedging in your crossbar. Don't use too much pressure; you may easily crack the container. However sturdy it looks, thick pottery can

*Suishin Kei arrangement of Nephrolepsis exaltata cristata and cymbidium orchids, in grey-green pottery bottle*

be as brittle as the thinnest glass, so use plenty of patience but very little force.

Most cylindrical Nageire containers, being hand-made, lack the strict precision of machine-made articles. The neck opening, for instance, may not be a true circle, or else it may be fractionally wider one inch down the neck than at the top. The same reservations apply to bamboo containers which are very popular for this kind of arrangement. Being a natural plant, bamboo rarely grows in a perfectly circular form. You must therefore inspect the inside of the container carefully before cutting the two sticks of the crossbar. The safest way is to face the container, decide where its front is, and identify it in some way. Cut your first stick to equal the outside diameter of the container's opening, and then tailor it very patiently, nibbling away at it with a sharp knife until it fits. Put it into position. Measure and cut the second stick in the same way. Meticulous arrangers often use sandpaper to rub away a superfluous fraction of an inch. Patience is essential, for a cracked container may be a disaster, and an ill-fitting Kubari is useless. When your crossbar is in position, you can start on the arrangement proper. Once again key the ends of your branches or flowers by cutting them to fit against the inside wall of the container. Try to confine your

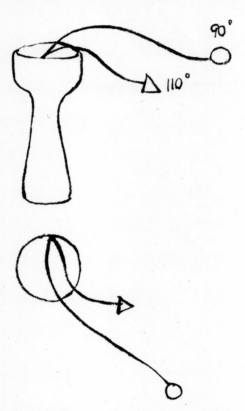

material to one quarter-section of the opening. For an Upright Style using branches, rest some of the stems against the centre of the crossbar. The longer the length of the stems below the crossbar, the higher the angle of your branches. If you are making an upright arrangement with flowers only, let the stems cross the container to fit against its inside wall on the opposite side of entry. For slanting and flat

arrangements put the branches under the crotch of the crossbar and make them fit neatly against the inside of the container.

Sometimes thin-stemmed flowers with heavy heads – e.g. carnations – tend to fall out of the vase. To prevent this, arrange them in your hand, tie the stems and trim the splayed ends to fit against the container. Similarly when short-stemmed flowers with heavy heads tend to slip out of a cascade-style arrangement, tie a long stick in the middle of their bunched stems. Key the end to rest against the inside wall.

*Fixing No. 3*

This method is particularly suitable for holding a heavy branch in position.

Having trimmed the branch, hold it firmly at the angle you want it to be at in the container; key it by cutting its base as in the previous methods. Then slice the stem horizontally with short, straight cuts for at least 3 in.

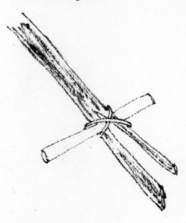

Cut a length of straight branch to fit across the inside of the container. With a knife flatten two long sides of it; the slit end of your heavy branch will fit more easily and more securely over a wedge than over a circle.

Insert this bar into the slit of your main branch

and tie them together with raffia in the criss-cross manner which allows you to scissor them through a narrow neck. Holding the branch upright in one hand, and with the other one manoeuvre the bar into the container. Whether you put it high or low depends on the angle at which you want your branch to stand. The length of the branch between its base and the bar will determine the angle at which it rises from the opening.

If possible, split your other branches to form diagonals inside the container; interlock them with the first fixing, or with the main branch which is already in position. Do not use too many fastenings. If your branches are properly keyed and cut, the first fixing will be sufficient to hold any other branches you wish to use.

There is an additional method for fixing an unusually heavy branch in a large exhibition arrangement. Key your branch to the side of the container and saw its base to the correct angle. Then choose a board which will go vertically inside the container, rather like a false lining, and nail your branch to it.

*Fixing No. 4*

This method, which is a combination of the vertical and horizontal fixing methods, is used for deep but wide, bulbous and odd-shaped containers.

A straight stick, slightly shorter than the container and placed in it off centre, will be the vertical fixing. For the horizontal one, cut a second stick to fit the container either across its greatest width or an inch below the neck.

*Suishin Kei arrangement "Spring".*
*Branches of Magnolia stellata in Old English glass bottle*

Cut the top of the vertical stick carefully down the centre for half its length. Generally speaking the length of the cut depends on the size of the container. In the same way slice one end of the horizontal stick. Should your shears have accidentally slipped off centre, let the stronger side of the split stick take the strain of interlocking.

Next, interlock the two sticks and tie them criss-cross fashion with bass. Once again this criss-cross binding enables you to scissor the two props through a narrow neck. Wedge the horizontal stick firmly in position. The vertical one should stand equally firmly on the base of the container.

Key your branches to fit against the inside of the container in the usual manner. They can go across the tie, through the split top of the vertical stick,

*Suishin Kei in a variety of dried materials, basket container*

or into the split end of the horizontal stick, the ends always resting against the inside of the container. This is a wonderful fixing method for a deep, drum-shaped container. I find that making the branches rise in a group from the outer edge and cross towards the centre gives a particular thrill. With this fixing, simple flowering branches can be arranged in a wide container of medium height. In addition to the four main fixing methods there is an additional one which can be described as a variation on the No. 2 – crossbar – method. It is chiefly used in classical containers, shaped like a Chinese ginger jar, to keep a branch or flower in an upright position.

Cut a stick to go across the bottom of the container and trim it to fit snugly. Flatten its sides to form a wedge. If you are using a branch, cut the end straight and slit it, then insert the wedge-shaped stick in the slit and tie with bass. If you are using a flower, tie its stem to the stick at about an inch from the bottom of the stem and then snip off the extra inch. This is easier than trying to tie the very end of the stem to the stick.

Next, measure the length of your branch or flower stem from the base to within $\frac{1}{2}$ in. of the neck of the container, and cut another stick to fit horizontally at that point. Tie this second stick to your branch or flower stem so that it is at right angles to the first stick at the bottom. In other words you now have a crossbar, its two halves divided by space but fulfilling a function similar to that of the No. 2 Fixing Method. Obviously if you use this method to keep your main

*Nageire form of Keishin Kei Variation No. 3*
*combining gladioli and Erica arborea in modern container*

*Risshin Kei, Variation No. 1    In Nageire container. Scots pine and white Lilium longiflorum.*
*Tall container is cinnamon-coloured with faint black markings*

line upright, your other branches and jushi will interlock with or balance against the first branch or flower fixed.

Using these fixings you can make all the styles you have learned in Moribana in Nageire-type containers. It is vitally important that you bear in mind that in all arrangements all measurements refer to the visible length of the stems only, i.e., the length that shows above the opening of the container.

This means that when you measure your Shin line, for instance, you must add to it the length of the stem which will be inside the container, and therefore invisible. Should your main branch go in the container to the depth of 6 in., for example, add the same number of inches to your main length.

Besides Risshin, Keishin and Haishin Kei, all of which are easily adapted to the "thrown-in" style, we also have a separate class of arrangements which are peculiar to Nageire. These belong to Suishin Kei, or the Hanging Style, which is a beautiful and elegant way of making flowers flow or cascade from a high point. Any of the Nageire fixing methods can be used in this style. Wall baskets and wells are popular for Suishin Kei arrangements, but tall containers are equally suitable.

In Suishin Kei arrangements the Shin line is always at an angle of $100°-120°$ from the imaginary vertical line rising from the centre of the container. Shin can change its position but not its angle. As in Haishin Kei, the other two main lines can change both angle and position, and their angles change from variation to variation.

*Nageire Suishin Kei arrangement of Viburnum fragrans and yellow Long Island chrysanthemums in Scandinavian glass container*

Let us start with the basic Suishin Kei, making an arrangement to sweep to the right. Generally speaking we imagine the opening of the container to be sectioned in the shape of St Andrew's Cross, which gives an open section each at the front and back, and on either side.

For a right-hand arrangement we shall use the left-hand section of the container. Shin starts from this section, goes to the left, returns low across the front of the container, and finishes at an angle of about 120°.

Leaving the container at the same point, Soe comes forward and then flows to the right at 90°. Hikae leaves the same section, goes towards the left, following the Shin line, and finishes at an angle of about 100°.

This being a basic arrangement, all lines flow forward; and being a right-hand one, they all start from the left-hand section of the opening.

The jushi rise slightly from the neck of the container so that the arrangement does not consist of falling lines only which could give it a rather unhappy look. Choose long jushi to follow Shin, and shorter ones rising slightly above the neck of the container to follow Hikae.

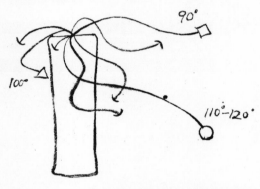

Now try another Suishin Kei arrangement, this time using the right-hand section of the neck of the container. Shin crosses the neck and falls in a semicircle, finishing on the left-hand side at an angle of 120°. Soe rises and follows the curve of Shin at 15°. Hikae goes to the right and dips below the edge of the neck, finishing at an angle of 100°.

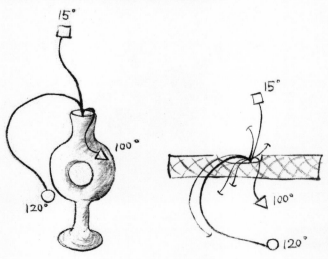

In the next variation Shin comes from the left of the container to the right front at 110°, Soe goes to the rear at 15°, Hikae to the right front at 35°, following the airy, open plan of Variation No. 1 and looking extremely pretty when made with sweet peas or morning glory.

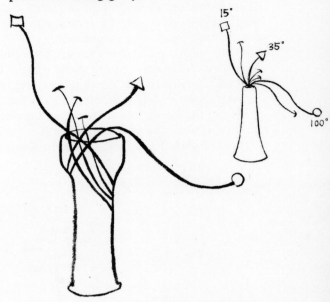

For a long, splayed look let Shin come down the front of the container at 120°. Soe goes to the back of the circle at 15°, and Hikae completes the triangle, rising at the centre and going right at 75°.

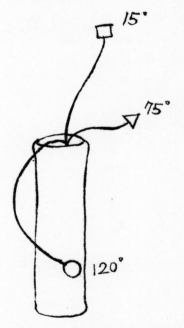

In yet another, remarkably elegant, variation both Shin and Soe leave the left-hand side of the container and turn to the left. Shin curves down and ends with its tip at 160° on the right. Soe curves to the right, returning to the left, and ending at 150°, at the left side of the container, while Hikae curves opposite Shin at 135° and stays on the same side. The jushi should cascade with abandon. Achieve balance by placing a large cluster of flowers or leaves at the neck of the container. All main lines will flow from this. This arrangement should only be made in a very tall and slender container.

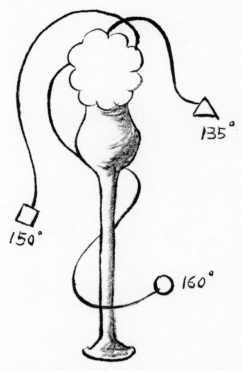

By now your attention to space and balance and your instinct for restraint will be so well developed that you will avoid all overcrowding or fussiness as a matter of course. Never forget that in all Suishin Kei arrangements the lines should hang but not droop.

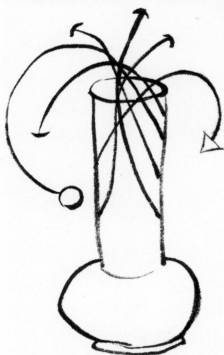

If you notice the slightest suggestion of drooping, adjust and place some jushi to rise slightly above the lip of the container. Alternately allow the jushi to join the cascading lines, but add a cluster of upward-pointing flowers or leaves at the neck of the container.

*Hanging Style arrangement.*
*Lichened larch branch and deep rose-coloured*
*amaryllis in a tall, off-white, textured container*

*Natural Style "Spring" arrangement consisting of almond blossom, branches of Spiræa arguta, and narcissi, in glass container*

# Chapter Eight

# Other Variations

Although Variations 7 and 8 are in many ways related to the earlier variations, they also have individual characteristics of their own which make it difficult to fit them easily into any of the previous styles; besides, their uses are rather special. For this reason, in my school I teach them separately.

*Variation No. 7*

This is divided into three distinct parts: Ukibana, or the Floating Arrangement; Shikibana, or the placing of flowering branches on a table without a container; and Morimono, an arrangement consisting of fruit or vegetables or both.

*Ukibana:* In Ukibana the water in the container serves as the background of the arrangement. It must, therefore, be crystal clear, and the pinholder, if used, immaculate. For my taste the container should be plain inside.

Water lilies and lotus flowers are a natural choice for a floating arrangement, but they will not stay open or indeed open at all, unless water is forced into them. The cellular stems prevent the water from being absorbed in the normal way.

Fill the syringe from your tool kit with fresh water; place the stem of the flower or leaf in the nozzle of the spray, and force water into it.

The individual sections of a link-type kenzan are excellent for holding your flowers slightly above the surface of the water. This is not so important with aquatic flowers such as the lotus and the water lily; which have a firm sheath below the flowers to hold the delicate petals clear of the water. Other flowers, not equipped by nature to float on water, tend to become water-logged after a while and lose their beauty as a result.

I have devised two ways of dealing with this problem, depending on whether the stem is an integral part of the design, or not.

In the first case the flower, whose stem has a role to play in the arrangement, must be kept in position, with its petals remaining dry. The way to achieve this while maintaining a natural look is to squeeze

the stem at about $\frac{1}{4}$ in. below the flower head, so that it can be bent without being broken. This $\frac{1}{4}$ in. of the stem is then impaled on the kenzan. This holds the flower just above the water which must, in all Ukibana arrangements, come to the top of the pins of the kenzan. The remainder of the stem lies horizontally along the water surface.

The round-nosed pliers used in basket making are ideal for squeezing the stems.

The leaves and their stems are anchored in the same way. The pattern would be destroyed if they were allowed to float freely.

In this arrangement the stem of Shin will measure three-quarters of the diameter of the container, the other stem lengths being in proportion. The angles will correspond precisely with those of the basic style elevations, the only difference being that instead of rising in the air, the lines are lying along the water surface.

Try this arrangement with scabious which may sound a most unlikely flower for a floating arrangement, but its stems with their fern-like leaves at the base create a striking effect in a large oval container.

As an alternative, used for flower heads with virtually no stem, I suggest, though not for the purist, small horseshoe shapes in plasticine, placed in the container to support the flower heads. The shape of the support allows the water to circulate freely around the stem, short though it is.

Try this arrangement with a tulip flower and a bud, adding a few camellia leaves as jushi. You may wish to rest a leaf on the edge of the container to avoid any impression of flatness.

Another version might be two gardenia flowers floating in a large black container; a camellia or orchid in a flat glass container, or possibly a frosted one to resemble a lump of ice.

*Shikibana:* Shikibana is the placing of branches and flowers directly on a table without a container. This is a charming way of decorating, and it is particularly suitable for a buffet party.

Of course, having no container means having no

water, and yet the plant material must be kept alive and fresh for several hours, perhaps in a hot, smoky atmosphere. To achieve this, I suggest that you wrap the stems of your flowers in tiny pieces of damp cotton wool and squeeze over them small pieces of baking foil. This will prevent both evaporation and damage to the furniture.

If the flowers do not have enough foliage to cover up the bright silver foil, use a piece of green oiled silk instead and tie it with matching thread. This may sound like a fiddling job but it is certainly worth the trouble.

*Morimono:* This is an arrangement made on a flat dish, basket, base or tray, in which the main lines are of fruit or vegetables or both. Flowers may be added as jushi, but they must be kept low. The use of kenzans and tall flowers would destroy the character of the arrangement.

As it would be both sad and wasteful to ruin a perfect peach or nectarine by impaling it on an orange stick, prevent your fruit from rolling out of position by fixing a small triangle of stems, where needed, to the flat tray or basket you are using as a container, and placing the fruit on it. These tiny bases will give ample support.

Choose fruit and vegetable for their colour and texture. Try using two apples with a few grapes, or two peaches with an orchid. Experiment with apricots, artichokes, lemons and aubergines. The range of possible combinations is endless. If you use fruits which have clearly defined "eyes" or stems, place them so that they do not all present the same aspect. Since the container serves as both background and frame for the arrangement, choose its colour with care, and place your material with a keen eye for space.

In a classical Morimono it is customary to represent the past, present, and future. A plant with carefully scrubbed roots would stand for the past, leaves for the present, and a chestnut in a split husk, or a fruit or seed, for the future. An arrangement on these lines should be placed on a maki-dai, i.e. a classical base in polished wood with turned-under ends. Another suggestion for the past-present-future arrangement, particularly suitable for the spring season, would feature a woodland violet or primrose plant with scrubbed roots which will not mark or soil the base. The flowers, being able to draw nourishment from the roots, will last for some time. You might add leaves and a few beech-nut husks or some fruit, for it is in the fruit that the seeds of the future lie.

*Variation No. 8*

This variation is a combination of two arrangements in one or two containers, each being complete in itself yet dependent on the other. Different materials may be used for each, so long as there is some link between them.

Throughout this variation, Shin of the second group should not exceed three-quarters of the length of Shin of the first group.

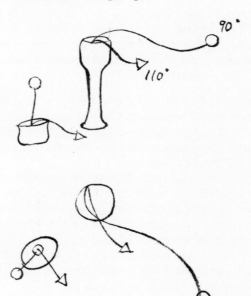

The basic arrangement in this variation is a combination of a Moribana and a Nageire, in whatever style your material dictates. Since you now have all the basic styles and their variations at your fingertips, one glance at a branch will tell you for which style and variation it is most suitable. It is this instinctive knowledge, and the ability to use it, which makes Ikebana so stimulating and enjoyable for the advanced student.

One version of this variation consists of two complete arrangements in one container. The kenzans must not be placed level with each other, and the seasonal rule of putting the larger group to the back in summer, and vice versa in winter, will apply.

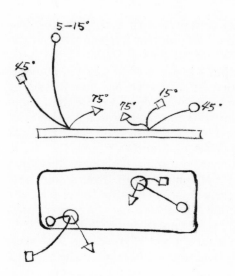

*Variation No. 8, representing "Spring" in the Natural Style,*
*consists of two complete arrangements in a deep brown*
*salt-glaze stoneware container by Rosemary Wren.*
*Lemon and white Daisy Schaffer daffodils.*
*The two wooden dolls add a country touch*

Another version, known as the "shadow" version, combines two different styles in two containers, one placed behind the other. Variation No. 3 of Keishin or Risshin Kei is placed at position five in the front container, and Variation No. 4 of Risshin Kei stands at its rear as the shadow in the second container. This variation can be interpreted in many different ways and with many different materials. Combine spring-flowering branches for the Keishin Kei No. 3, and pussywillow and tuberose for the basic upright; or sprays of spiraea for the front group, and the elegant iris with its beautiful leaves for the rear one. The following versions may be termed "mass", or "solid", arrangements.

In one we use a pair of containers, one standing slightly behind the other, and make two blocks of

*"Shadow" variation combining Nos. 3 and 4, iris and Nephrolepsis exaltata cristata in two matching containers*

colour with flowers. Let your eye guide you in finding the correct height for Shin of the first group. Personally I like to leave a little gap between the tip of Shin and the supporters which are then built up into a solid but balanced mass, accentuating, if possible, the natural line of Shin. Since Shin of the secondary group would measure three-quarters of the length of Shin of the main group, this makes the secondary group at the rear shorter and, as a result, somewhat lighter.

This arrangement looks particularly attractive if you use tall flowers such as stocks, delphiniums or larkspur, the florets of which are by nature tightly packed. It also looks attractive with iris and carnations. All the flowers should be of the same type, but different colours are permitted.

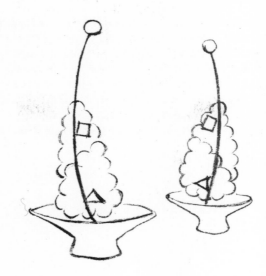

*Carnations in subtly shaded colours arranged in two stoneware containers "Block Buster"*

In another version the arrangement is made in a Moribana container by combining two geometrical shapes – one upright column and one L-shaped mass, for example, the first being in foliage, the second in flowers. Or use flowers for the main group, and a mass of foliage and colour for the secondary group. This arrangement depends on colour, shape and texture, and not on individual flowers.

## The "Sketch of Nature" Group

This is common to all schools; the Sogetsu School calls it a sketch of nature. It is a particularly enjoyable arrangement for city dwellers who may have little opportunity of enjoying the changing seasons, except by observing the clouds and the sky. This arrangement can, to a limited extent, bring flowers, trees and a touch of the seasons to the most urban home.

The first arrangement in this "Sketch of Nature" group is known to my students and myself as Masami One. Masami, my delightful Japanese assistant, is a teacher of Ikebana, and when she made this arrangement in one of her classes, my students were so delighted that they decided to name it in the school curriculum as Masami One.

For this you need a Moribana container, two kenzans, some moss, and five groups of flowers and leaves. Daffodils or other spring flowers are a suitable choice for it.

Place the kenzans in the container, one to the left and one to the right; they should not be level. Between them they will hold five flower groups. The first and second groups consist of a bud and four leaves each, and groups 3, 4 and 5 of a full flower and four leaves each. As the length of Shin of group No. 1 should equal the diameter of the container, you may have to choose your container according to the length of the flower stems. Group No. 2 should measure two-thirds of No. 1, and Nos. 3, 4 and 5 will be graded from No. 2, getting progressively shorter.

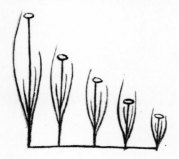

Ideally, for this arrangement you need spring daffodils or narcissi growing in a sheath with their leaves. You may be fortunate enough to find them in this condition at your florist's; if you grow your own flowers, cut them so that the sheath remains intact. You will find that each sheath varies, some with as many as six leaves with each flower, but as you only need four leaves and one flower or bud for your groups, you will have to take the natural group apart and reassemble it.

To do this, squeeze the stems in the sheath very firmly between your fingers with a rolling action; bruise them, in fact. This will loosen them without splitting the sheath. Take out first the flower and then the leaves one by one. I prefer to allow one leaf to remain in the sheath to hold it open. As the sheath is very delicate and splits easily, this operation needs skill and a gentle touch.

Having taken flower and leaves out of the sheath, reassemble them. Each flower or bud is to have four leaves of uneven length, so that to the left of the flower there will be a long one and, next to that, a short one, and to the right of the flower a very short one and a very long one. To achieve this, put back first the two outer leaves into the sheath, then the two inner ones, and, last of all, the flower. Leave the sheath an inch or so up the stem; the purpose of this is to keep the leaves close to the flower stems.

If you have not been fortunate enough to find flowers complete with their natural sheath, make your own by assembling the group as described above, and bind the stems for about 1 in. with bass, tying and trimming the ends.

Now place your groups on the two kenzans. If No. 1 is placed on a kenzan on the left side of the arrangement, it will look diagonally to the right. No. 2 will go at the centre back of the second kenzan and look diagonally to the left. No. 3 will stand at the outside of No. 1, No. 4 will be on the outside of No. 2, and No. 5 will be on the inside of No. 1. You have, in fact, made a grouping of three and two, and turned the faces of your groups to give a natural impression.

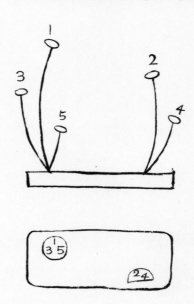

Now cover your kenzans and the base of your container with moss, having first carefully removed from its surface every tiny piece of leaf or twig which might look untidy.

Create extra interest by building up a hummock here and there, putting moss on moss. This will make your daffodils look as if they were growing on an undulating woodland bank. Do not let the water cover the moss.

The second nature sketch, known as Masami Two, is a little more elaborate. It can be interpreted either as a land scene or a water scene. The grouping of the former is similar to that of Masami One. You will need a large flat container and five kenzans.

The land scene in Masami Two consists of five groups. No. 1, the tallest, is a branch; No. 2, being two-thirds of the height of No. 1, is a group of seasonal flowers; No. 3 a group of leaves; No. 4 a short branch supported by flowers, and No. 5 flowers supported by a short branch.

The positions of the groups are similar to those of Masami One. The first group goes to the right-hand rear corner, the second group a little way in from the left-hand rear corner, the third group is standing at the base of the first, the fourth a little inside from the second, and the fifth to the front of the second. If you are doing a "spring garden", a spray of woodland cyclamen or violets will look attractive at the base of Nos. 2 and 4. Do not put them at the base of all groups; this would overcrowd the arrangement.

Cover the base of the container with moss, but leave

*"Sketch of Nature" arrangement referred to in text as Masami One.*
*Daffodils and moss in a flat, rectangular container*

one corner free. This is to give the impression that the land in your land scene finishes at the edge of the water.

Equally, if you are making a water scene, using aquatic plants, reeds, bulrushes, water lilies, etc., make a small corner as a land group with a blossoming branch, and cover this land section with moss. Or, to indicate the spot where the land begins, place there a large stone as a cliff face.

A water scene with a "tree" coming from the land over the water is called a *kansuiki*, i.e. a water-viewing arrangement. The idea is that the branch is looking over the water from the land, with the sunlight coming through its leaves and being reflected in the water. This arrangement is peculiar to spring and summer.

*Mobiles*

The next step, the making of mobiles, marks an entirely new departure. A mobile is an arrangement of natural and/or artificial materials. It can be made of grasses and flowers, small wooden ships, autumn berries, cut-to-pattern bamboos, or, indeed, of absolutely anything. Its essence is that it is suspended by one thread and subsequently each object is separately balanced. Both objects and sections must be light enough to move freely, and designed to be able to revolve without touching.

I always start a mobile by wedging the end of a slender bamboo stem or a piece of wire with a heavy weight to keep it from swinging, and then making my mobile in groups of Shin, Soe and Hikae. First the Shin group is balanced, lifted, and put under the

*"Sketch of Nature" arrangement, Masami Two, consisting of jonquils, chrysanthemums, evergreen pine and spring-flowering branches*

*Opposite page*
*Mobile consisting of driftwood, dried yellow South African daisies and rust-coloured grass*

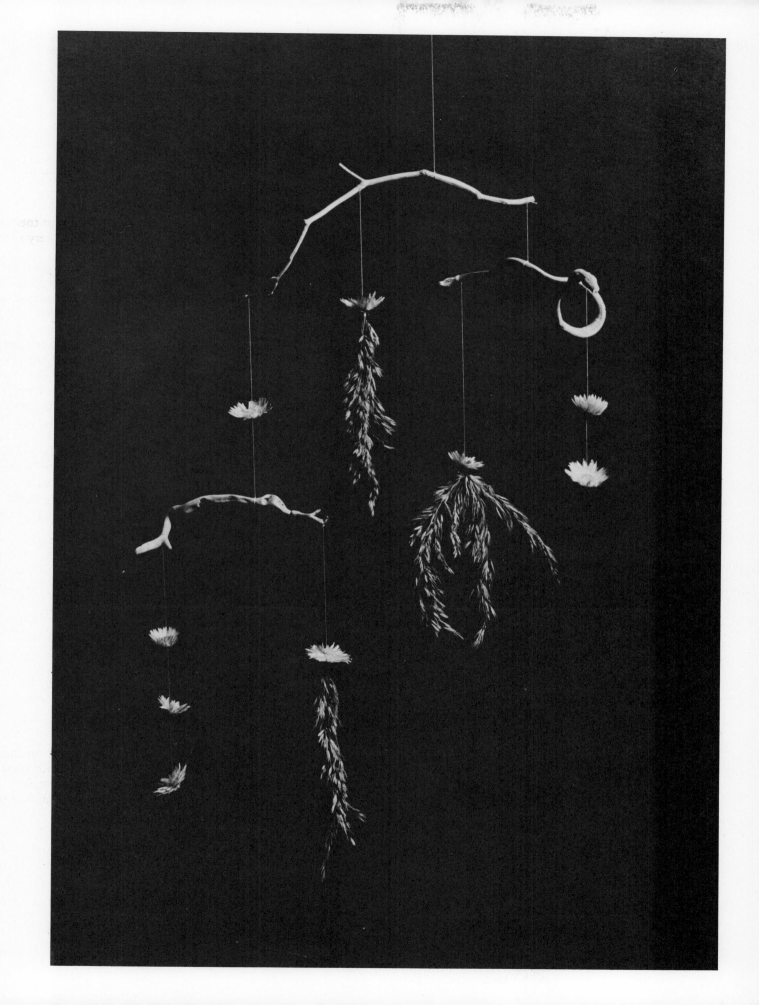

weight; then the Soe group, and finally the Hikae group. The crossbars or struts are made of light but strong wood or wire, and tied to the main support with fishing line or silk.

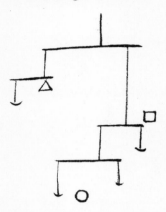

Once balance has been achieved, the fishing line or silk must be knotted carefully and the knot secured with a tiny blob of glue. Nothing is more frustrating than to find the threads slipping along the bars, causing the painstakingly balanced mobile to tip and even collapse.

You can make exciting large-scale mobiles with lanterns for a summer party in the garden. They are also great fun to make for children's playgrounds or rooftop terraces. The scope is infinite, with plenty of room for individual ideas. The easiest mobile to make is one consisting of balls and paper shapes, the latter folded or cut according to the rules of Origami and Kirigami, the Japanese arts of paper folding and cutting. Incidentally, Origami is a wonderful way to keep children amused. Kirigami, which requires scissors, is perhaps more suitable for older children.

*Reliefs*

Now try your hand at reliefs. A relief is a collage. A composition of berries, twigs, dry seed-pods, egg-shells, seaweed, or any similar material is made in a picture frame or shallow wooden box, and then plaster is carefully poured in so that it is set in position.

You can produce a small relief by pouring the plaster in first and then making your composition. But plaster sets very quickly, in three minutes or so, which does not leave much time for placing your components. To my mind the best method is to have two frames made – one with, and one without a bottom. This allows you to make up your composition in the bottomless frame, getting every detail correct so that there is no need for last-moment alterations. Then you pour the plaster in the other frame and quickly transfer the pieces in the correct order from the first one.

For a start, use a small lid. A wooden one from a box of Turkish delight is ideal for the purpose. Pour plaster in it and start making miniature pictures using pussywillow, buds, stems, small berries and beech nuts. Making small natural scenes of this kind will allow you to master the technique so that you

can graduate to larger frames and make pictures. Your best relief may eventually take pride of place in your home. It is essentially a temporary form of art, but with a good technique and some creative talent the most exciting objects can be made.

My Japanese teacher made collages by rolling the colourful, highly patterned pages of *Life* Magazine into fine rolls, rather like pipe cleaners, and then methodically sticking or pasting them within her frame to form designs. She achieved marvellous results.

Another intriguing method is to cover a piece of board with velvet and then thread brightly coloured silks between upholstery studs; this makes a striking picture.

Because plaster sets so quickly, very large reliefs are usually made by groups of people. This is a good exercise in teamwork, and great fun, too. Remember that plaster is very heavy; $\frac{3}{8}$ in. is all the thickness you need for a relief. Hammer small tacks at irregular intervals into the background to key your plaster to it.

Finally in these extra variations there is the kake-bana, an arrangement to be hung on the wall in a light container, such as a bamboo or a basket. Obviously this arrangement must be light, and not protrude too far into the room.

To achieve flowing lines, the material will be fixed into position by one of the kubari mentioned in the chapter on Nageire. It is the custom in Japan to hang the kake-bana on a kake-ita, which is a board or mat specially designed for the purpose of protecting the wall.

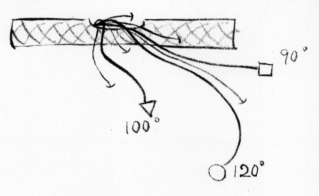

A kake-bana is an ideal arrangement for spring and summer. Use clematis or morning glory, with some of the trailing ferns. Generally speaking the simple basic arrangements are best. For this Suishin Kei is, of course, a popular choice.

*Opposite page*
*Combination arrangement, Variation No. 8*
*Narcissus Cheerfulness and its leaves*
*on two kenzans in a square black container*

*Sogetsu Rikkwa depicting the four seasons
made by Sofu Teshigahara in London in October 1965*

# Chapter Nine

# Classical Arrangements

Classical arrangements are in a category of their own, and are subject to their own rules.

Originally, schools of Ikebana were either classical or modern. In Japan the classical schools have now added modern arrangements to their syllabus, while the modern ones have adapted classical arrangements to contemporary requirements. As a result, it is possible to see a Rikka made in the modern style by a master of a modern school; in 1965, Mr Teshigahara delighted London audiences with such an arrangement which was 15 ft. high and depicted the seasons of the year.

Although the styles intermingled, each school has retained its individual characteristics, so that a Sogetsu student could recognize Mr Teshigahara's modern Rikka as a Sogetsu arrangement. In the same way a modern arrangement made, for instance, by Mr Ikenobo, would impress a student of Ikenobo as clearly belonging to that school.

Many years ago, before this happy reconciliation of the old and new, a student would choose one school at which he or she wished to study, and remain faithful to it. Later it became acceptable to study at both a modern and a classical school. Nowadays this is no longer necessary, since many schools cover every aspect of Ikebana. Of the three principal schools the Sogetsu is noted for its modern approach, the Ikenobo for its traditional, and the Ohara for its natural approach.

The earliest classical arrangements were in the Rikka Style, which developed into the Seika or Shoka Style.

There are nineteen different variations of classical Rikka arrangements. In most of them the branches and flowers are held in place by being inserted in the centre of a tightly tied bunch of straw, or into tubes held in place by the straw. The arrangement is always placed in the centre of the container. In the upright variations tall, urn-shaped containers are used. The flat variations are known as sand arrangements and are made in the suna-bachi or sand bowl. They are always broader than they are high. The suna-bachi itself is a deep, rectangular shape with a

false top which is covered with $\frac{1}{2}$ in. of sand.

The rigidity of the rules for Rikka is well illustrated by the fact that out of the nineteen variations, seven consist of one kind of material only. Special instructions are given for the use of pine, cherry blossom, Japanese iris, narcissus, chrysanthemum, maple and lotus.

The lotus, for instance, which is the emblem of Buddhism, symbolizes many virtues, among them sincerity, nobility, elegance and, above all, purity, because the lotus flower rises from the muddy bottom of the lake without being besmirched, and opens up in immaculate beauty above the water. In every classical lotus arrangement the three phases of existence are represented; the past by the seed head, the present by the open flower, and the future by the bud and the folded leaves.

The other variations of Rikka are combinations of specifically named material.

In Rikka the length of the Shin branch can be from three to six times the height or breadth of the container, which makes for rather tall or broad effects. The supporting branches are cut according to the length of Shin. All the branches are in set positions. The back of the arrangement should be of as much interest as the front.

Modern Japanese Rikka arrangements are limited only by the creative ability of the arranger, but traditional ones were always subject to strict rules governing the line, the combination of plants, and the occasions on which specific plants had to be used.

For many years now the traditional stereotyped Rikka form has been considered outdated and totally unsuited to modern life. But the proliferation of monumental office blocks with their austere lines has created a new rôle and an ideal background for modern Rikka arrangements.

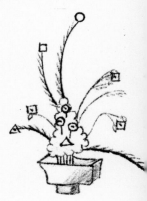

In the Modern School the rules for classical arrangements in general are flexible. There are three styles – the formal, semi-formal and informal which are upright, slanting and flat, respectively. The rules for these are peculiar to each style.

For classical arrangements of the Seika or Shoka type, the kenzan or kubari is placed in the centre of the container. The branches are carefully trimmed and shaped to rise as one for the first few inches above the rim of the container.

A special kubari or wooden support is used to achieve this look of unity.

To make this, cut a stick to fit across the neck of the container about 1 in. below the top. With short, straight cuts slit it for approximately one-third of its length, and tie it with bass at the end of the cut to prevent further splitting.

You will also need a komi, a pliable stick somewhat shorter than the diameter of the container, to "lock" your branches when they are in position.

Fix the kubari, into position, opening the slit so that you have a Y shape, the slit end being at the rear, opposite you.

*Opposite page*
*Basic formal arrangement of three lines.*
*Irish yew branches in dark green and blue*
*container, with white pebbles*

The branches for this arrangement should form graceful curves, so it is best to choose supple ones – for example pussywillow, dogwood, Irish yew, broom or grevillea. Later when you have mastered the technique, you may experiment with roses, chrysanthemums and other plants which have less pliable stems.

As a rule the Shin branch will measure twice the length of the container, Soe will be three-quarters of Shin, and Hikae three-quarters of Soe.

It is easy to differentiate between the three variations of these arrangements if you remember that in the formal the longest line is in the upright position; in the semi-formal it is in the slanting position, and in the informal it is in a low or flat position. The angles in a formal arrangement are $5°$ for Shin, $45°$ for Soe, and $75°$ for Hikae.

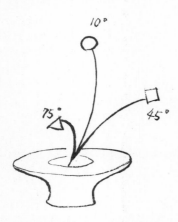

Select and cut your branches to the correct lengths. Trim the base of each to about one-third of its length, removing all buds and protuberances, so that the stems will lie together. This length of combined stems below the point where the branches diverge is called the nemoto.

Take all three branches in your hands, holding them with your thumbs underneath and fingers above, and bend them gently but firmly until they form graceful curves, but leave the nemoto straight. The next step is to "key" the branches by cutting the ends to fit against the side of the container, and to place them one by one in the kubari.

Start with Soe. Key it first, then place it to the front of the crotch of the kubari so that it comes towards your left shoulder, with its tip at an angle of $45°$. Now lock Soe into position with the komi, which is your secondary support.

Key Shin, take out the komi and place Shin in position in the kubari at an angle of $5°$. Its tip should return to a point almost vertically above its base. Replace the komi.

Finally key Hikae, take out the lock and place Hikae in the kubari, making it come from the back towards your right shoulder, at an angle of $75°$. Replace the komi. Hold the nemoto in position with one hand, and with the other complete your bending; remove unnecessary leaves and make final adjustments.

In the fundamental styles one seldom makes an arrangement consisting of branches only; it is more usual to use branches for the main lines and add flowers as jushi. But in the classical arrangements tree branches are frequently used on their own, especially those of flowering trees such as the cherry, peach and plum, which are rarely used once blossom time is over.

If instead of strong, leafy branches you wish to use material with long, single stems, Prunus triloba, for instance, form groups for each main line by taking three stems for Shin, two for Soe and three for Hikae.

I find this grouping of lines very helpful when I make an arrangement with the straight, rather thin branches of my peach tree in the spring. The precious blossoms look so lovely in this style that I leave the pruning until the tree is in bud. It does not seem any the worse for it, perhaps because it gets an extra-generous mulching in the summer as a thank you.

*Classical arrangement of yellow narcissi in a salt-glaze container*

This classical arrangement can also be made with multi-flowered jonquils which have been "goo-ed" and reassembled. "Gooing" is an unorthodox term which we adopted for lack of a better one, to describe a certain process.

To "goo" jonquils, lay them on a pad of newspaper and stroke their stems from flower head to base firmly, but not harshly, with the side of your shears, pushing out all the glutinous "goo" substance from the stems. Incidentally, this treatment should only be used on jonquils. It does not suit hollow-stemmed flowers.

Placing two leaves of varying length at either side of the flower stem, make five individual groups, each one consisting of one flower and four leaves of unequal length. Tie the base of each group, and again two-thirds of the way up with bass, using a quick-release knot for the latter. Lay the groups in a shallow dish of iced water for at least an hour. When you make the arrangement, take up the groups in turn and place them in the kubari, following the same method as before. You will find that the stems are firm and the flowers fresh, and that they will remain so for several days. When you have completed the arrangement to your satisfaction, remove the top ties.

Classical arrangements can be made on a kenzan, but it is not easy to keep the branches and flowers in position. You will find that using the kubari is both easier and more satisfactory.

The semi-formal and informal variations only differ from the formal in the positions of the main lines. Another attractive group is that of the boat arrangements which express various meanings, such as welcome, farewell, patience and prosperity. Among them we find the outward-going boat or defune, the homeward-going boat or irefune, sailing in the mist or oki-orai, sailing towards the beach or nagisai-orai, the boat at anchor or oki-fune, and swift sailing.

In early arrangements the direction of the outward- or homeward-going boat depended on the placing of the tokonoma in the Japanese home. But nowadays when fewer and fewer tokonomas are built, it is generally accepted that the outward-bound boat sails to the left and the homeward-bound to the right.

To speed a departing guest, one would make a defune or outward-going boat. The kenzan will be in the centre, the bows to the left. Shin will measure approximately twice the length of the container, Soe three-quarters of Shin, Hikae three-quarters of Soe.

Shin and Soe are curved to resemble sails. Shin stands at the centre-back of the kenzan, its tip returning to 5° beyond the vertical zero line. Soe stands at the left front, supporting Shin, with its tip ending just short of the zero line, at 45°. Hikae stands at the right front of the kenzan, supporting the line of Soe and Shin at the base, its tip coming to a point just to the right of the zero line, at 75°. In this arrangement two long, slender branches will be used for oars, placed on the kenzan at the right-hand side, behind Hikae. They clear the edge of the "boat" and dip into the "water". The jushi will be light and high to symbolize a light heart and good wishes, supporting the main lines within their confines. All lines are inclined to the front to give a feeling of movement.

Reverse this arrangement to make an irefune, or homeward-bound boat. The bows are to the right, and the jushi are low and darker in colour, since a well-laden boat would sit low in the water – the symbol of a successful journey and prosperity.

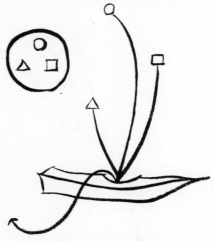

Irefune is often used as a welcome-home arrangement. Oki-fune or boat at anchor is the only arrangement in this group which is placed on a base; rightly so, for it is the only boat not under way. This arrangement denotes good sense and patience, because the boat is waiting and will not leave its safe anchorage until the storm has subsided.

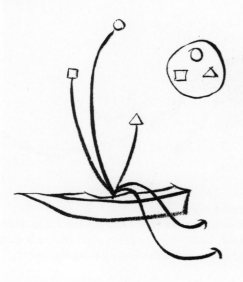

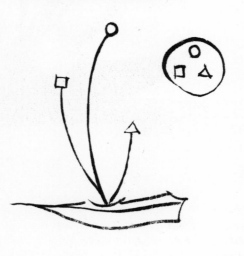

The main lines symbolize furled sails and will therefore be upright. Shin will be twice the length of the boat, Soe and Hikae being in the usual proportions.

The kenzan is placed in the centre of the container. Shin, in the upright position, stands at the centre back of the kenzan. Soe supports Shin on the left or right, according to the direction of the bows. Hikae stands beside Shin opposite to Soe, on the stern. Jushi should be placed within the outline formed by the main branches. If you add a streamer, it will be long and slender, representing the anchor rope.

Oki-orai, or sailing in the mist, represents a romantic boat on the horizon. It has an air of mystery, and, being at an imagined distance, its main lines are not very clearly defined. This arrangement looks very

attractive if made in pine branches, gypsophila or maidenhair fern with flowers in bud, or small flowers. The angles, proportions and positions of the main lines are as in the outward- or homeward-bound boat.

The swift sailing is an exciting boat arrangement in which branches with exaggerated curves are used to represent billowing sails. In this version Shin will measure at least twice the length of the container; Soe will be three-quarters of Shin, and Hikae one-half of Soe.

Shin stands at the centre back of the kenzan. It curves towards the bows and doubles back on itself until its tip is almost over the stern. Soe supports Shin. It is also curved, with its tip stopping short of the zero line. Hikae follows the general curve of

*Above*
*Boat arrangement. Salix glandulosa setsuka and pink tulips in a black container*

*Opposite page*
*Homeward-bound boat arrangement. Blue cedar branches and dark red roses, kept low indicating that the treasure-laden boat sits low in the water*

Shin and Soe, standing opposite Soe on the kenzan, but its tip returns to the Shin side of the zero line. A long streamer rests on the surface of the imaginary sea, going beyond the tip of Shin to accentuate the long horizontal line of the main branches. The jushi are compact, following the lines of Shin and Soe. All lines come forward to give the impression of swift sailing.

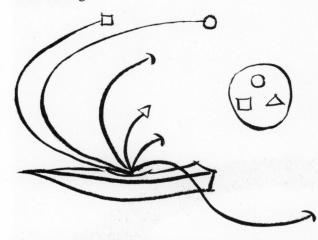

Early boat arrangements were hung in the tokonoma, at a height where the water in the containers could not be seen; water in a boat suggested a sinking ship and was considered an ill omen. These old traditions endure; even today many flat-bottomed boat containers, made for standing, have a decking to cover the water.

Another delightful category of classical arrangements expresses the cycles of the moon – waxing, full and waning. These arrangements are made in moon-shaped containers, with the kenzan in the centre and all lines coming forward.

Only one side of the container is used. The waxing moon, which is bright and full of promise, is often made with branches of plum blossom, wistaria, clematis and vines. All lines flow to the left of the container. The nature of the material used will generally dictate the angles. Try to achieve a curved but uncrowded line, with simplicity as its keynote. For a full-moon arrangement make an upright grouping in the centre of the moon container so that all lines remain within its inner circle. Try making it in flowers only, using tulips, irises or tree peony flowers with their foliage.

I remember an exquisite moon arrangement which I saw at an Ikebana exhibition one Christmas. With ilex, one of the less prickly kinds, for main lines, and Christmas roses for jushi, the arrangement had a purity and tranquillity which was outstanding amid the conventional glitter of other seasonal efforts. A waning moon arrangement should look pale and lonely. It is often made with sparse material, sometimes with grasses. The kenzan is placed in the centre and all lines go from the front to the right-hand side of the container, often trailing.

Finally, there is the traditional flower arrangement known as chabana, made for the tea ceremony. One branch and/or one flower is deemed to be sufficient. Often the camellia, which is considered one of the most difficult plants to arrange effectively, is used. For the chabana you will wish to achieve, you will need a long, pure line, a bud and a full

flower. You must then turn these into an object of exquisite loveliness. If you look at a freshly cut camellia branch, you will see that although this, too, has a certain beauty of its own, it lacks the elegance required in a chabana. To achieve this, you must study the branch, remove all superfluous flowers, leaves and small side branches, and then bend it carefully to the required line. This is a true shibui (supremely elegant) arrangement for which there are no formal rules, but in which the delicacy of the line and the beauty of the flower in itself are paramount.

*Opposite page*
*Classical arrangement of "boat at anchor".*
*Pale pink gladioli in black "boat" container,*
*green inside*

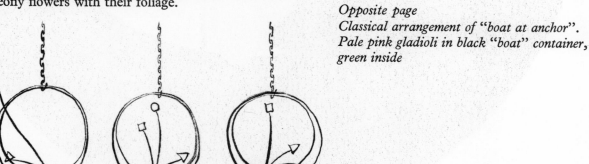

*Below*
*Classical "Full Moon" arrangement of Anthurium andreanum, in a black "moon" container*

*Opposite*
*Classical arrangement of Strelitzia reginae with its own leaves in circular container*

*Free Style arrangement for winter consists of berried holly branches and Helleborus niger, arranged in a pair of Japanese snow shoes*

*A phantasy: Rain*

*Previous page*
*Girls Festival Arrangement*
*Prunus triloba and Yellow Freesia*
*in modern black container*

*Opposite page*
*Eremurus, Agapanthus*
*and Eryngium*
*arranged by Masami*

*Below*
*Haishin Kei No. 6, Odontoglossum, Orchids*
*on a gold tray with leaves of Chlorophytum*
*plant*

*Top left*
*The Tanabata Kosiwai arrangement*
*of bamboo, oregami and irigami*

*Bottom left*
*Free style arrangement "Mist" consists of*
*massed blue irises with black thorny branches*
*of Aegle sepiaria, to suggest mist rising*
*over water. Two black metal containers*

*Above*
*Modern arrangement using cat-tails and South African*
*berries—an exercise in line*

*Right*
*An arrangement of black reeds and flame-coloured summer*
*cypruss portrays the ever-growing flame of Ikebana*
*International in honour of its founder Ellen Gordon Allen*

*Opposite page*
*Nageire—the vertical and horizontal fixing used to*
*support peregrine peach branches in fruit.*
*Modern matt glaze container*

*Below*
*An abstract arrangement using swarf, wood*
*and coloured balls*

*Autumn Splendour
Pyracantha . . .
arranged with a root in a salt-glazed
stoneware container*

*The seven grasses of Autumn
This arrangement uses seven different materials
gathered from the countryside.
The wooden dolls are made by
country craftsmen*

# Chapter Ten

# Free Style

Let us assume that by now you have become familiar with your plant material; you understand its characteristics and know how to handle it. Working with various materials in all phases of their development and at different times of the year will have taught you to enjoy the seasons as they come round.

The styles you have studied so far have all followed the dictates of nature quite closely. This is why they are known as the natural styles. As you know, the aim of these was to reproduce nature faithfully in the microcosm of an arrangement; every aspect of your work, from the choice and combination of materials to the angles at which certain flowers grow in their original state, was regulated by the laws of natural plant life.

The time has now come for you to go beyond nature's rules and regulations and test your creative ability in the Free Style. This is a very important part of your Ikebana training; it serves as a transition stage between the Natural and the Modern Styles. As a teacher I find that most students have difficulty in proceeding from the strictly regulated natural styles to the comparative freedom of the Modern, and the complete freedom of the Abstract and Avant-Garde Styles, the last of which can embrace materials as artificial and as wide-ranging as wire, glass and metal, and in which the absence of rules may easily cause the student to lose all restraint and the necessary respect for balance, accent and space.

This is why I advocate the Free Style as a valuable halfway house between the Natural and Modern Styles. It gives fuller scope to your artistic instinct and talent than the earlier sections, while permitting the use of natural materials contrary to their nature. Yet at the same time it is based on the principle of three, and this provides the beginner with some useful discipline.

The elementary Free Style diagrams are meant to guide your first steps. Beyond that you must use your own judgement and allow your eye, mind and imagination to develop in preparation for the Modern Style.

To make any Free Style arrangement, take two fundamental variations, choose a main characteristic of each, and combine them in a harmonious whole. Let us, for instance, combine Variations 1 and 2 of the Upright Style. The main characteristic of No. 1 is the open spaciousness of the arrangement. To emphasize this, the kenzan is placed to the front of the container, Shin making use of the back section of the horizontal circle which surrounds the kenzan. The main characteristic of No. 2 is that Soe is at an angle of 75°.

Combine the two in a left-hand Free Style arrangement. Place your kenzan in position No. 1. Shin goes back diagonally to the right at 5°–15°. Soe comes from the left front of the kenzan out of the container, continuing the Shin line and pointing beyond your left shoulder, at an angle of 75°. Hikae stands to the right front of the kenzan and rises diagonally to the right, at an angle of 45°, supporting Shin.

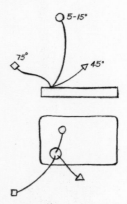

Jushi are placed to accent a line. Space is jealously guarded.

It must be remembered that in Free Style arrangements much more is left to the student's creative talent and artistic imagination than in the natural styles. But for a start I shall give a few suggestions for suitable plant material, and for our first arrangement you might like to use blackthorn branches for Shin, Soe and Hikae, and nine blue irises as supporters. To produce a sense of unity,

82

"The Mad Umbrella" Free Style arrangement of Salix glandulosa
setsuka branch, with Lilium longiflorum, in orange matt-glaze container

other jushi will consist of short pieces of blackthorn.
Support Hikae with your first jushi, and support
that with a second, shorter one in the centre between
Hikae and Soe; give Soe a very long supporting
jushi, and Shin a very short one at the base. Add an
extra dimension to your arrangement with a "shadow"
standing in the two-o'clock position to Shin. "Recess"
the rest of the iris in the centre of the arrangement,
but be careful to leave an accent on space, which in
this case would be between Shin and Soe.
Now let us combine Variations 5 and 6 in the Flat
Style. The main characteristic of No. 5 is that it is a
kabuwaki, a divided arrangement; of No. 6, that it
is designed to be viewed from four sides.
Combining the two in the Free Style calls for two
kenzans. Let us use the two parts of a sun-and-moon

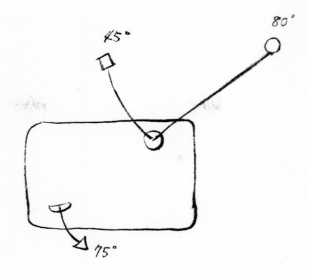

*Free Style arrangement of Salix, pine and red Baccarat roses*
*in a red-and-white Iwata container. Salix tied in circle as boomerang*

type, which surely was invented for divided arrangements. The main kenzan goes to position No. 3, with Shin moving to the right rear, at an angle of 80°, and Soe, placed on the kenzan opposite Shin, going to the left rear, at 45°. Hikae is on the second kenzan which is placed at the front of the container in position No. 1. It comes to the front, at 75°.

As this arrangement is to be viewed from four sides, the jushi in the main group will be long to support Shin, and very short to support Hikae; some short jushi may come from the back of Shin and cross towards your Hikae group. The Hikae jushi will be short, supporting Hikae to the front, but there may be long jushi on the secondary kenzan extending towards and supporting Soe which is on the main kenzan. This subtle linking of the two groups across the water promotes the unity of the arrangement.

Try this arrangement using deep red Baccarat roses for your main lines and some of your jushi, and snow-white chrysanthemums for your other jushi. As the festival colours are red and white in Japan, this makes a beautiful and appropriate celebration arrangement.

It can also be made in two containers, placing them very close, but not level with one another.

Another interesting possibility is to combine Variations 5 and 3 in the Upright Style. No. 5,

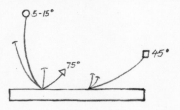

*Free Style arrangement. Cornus alba sibirica and Pink King protea with croton leaves in blush-white container*

kabuwaki, means dividing the arrangement; No. 3 is to be viewed from three sides, with one main branch coming directly to the front from the centre front of the pinholder.

For a Free Style combination of these two, place your main kenzan to the left front of the container. Shin rises from the left front of the kenzan, at an angle of 15°. Hikae is placed on the kenzan opposite Shin and comes directly forward, at 75°. Soe, on the second kenzan which is placed at the right rear of the container, crosses the latter towards your right shoulder, at 45°.

As in this version both Shin and Hikae are on the main kenzan, we must follow the direction normally given for the Omission Style variations, so that, should we wish to add a long jushi to Shin, this must go at its rear, to one side, as if it were a tall "shadow"; otherwise it might confuse the line by appearing to be a Soe between Shin and Hikae. Support Hikae with jushi. The jushi of the second

*Opposite page*
*Arrangement of eucalyptus and Lapageria rosea, in modern black double-necked container*

group should be short, although supporting Soe, which is the "lonely one", and should conceal the kenzan.

Another very popular Free Style arrangement is the combination of No. 1 and 2, Keishin Kei, which is often called the Back Style of No. 1.

As you know, Variation 1 is characterized by its openness, while Variation 2 is the only arrangement in which Hikae goes to the rear. The position of the kenzan for a right-hand Variation is the left front corner of the container.

Shin stands at the centre front of the kenzan, coming towards your left shoulder, at an angle of 15°. Soe stands at the right rear of the kenzan and goes away from Shin to the right rear of the container, at an angle of 45°. Hikae stands at the left rear of the

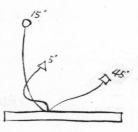

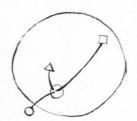

kenzan, opposite Soe, and goes towards the centre rear, at an angle of 5°.

This is a marvellous arrangement for showing the beauty of the backs of flowers, in particular of the arum lily. As the flower for Shin is placed in the upright position, slightly turning its face, you can see the beauty of its throat. The position and angle of Soe display the lovely neck of the flower, and Hikae, although at the back, allows us to see the classical outline of the lip of the flower. If you choose arum lilies, use two of their leaves as jushi; all you need to add is a few stones to cover the kenzan.

Try this arrangement also with chrysanthemums; it will bring into full effect the beauty of their calyxes and the reverse of their petals. Their own leaves will make satisfactory jushi. But as an alternative use large, light-coloured chrysanthemums for your main lines, and smaller flowers in a darker shade for jushi; in this case the jushi should stand in the centre and support Hikae. Their lengths should be about half of that of the branch they support.

Another variation which I like very much is Free Style No. 4.

As you know, No. 4 is an Omission Style, using the Heaven and Earth branches and omitting the Man branch. In Free Style No. 4 we omit Earth as well, which leaves us with Heaven alone. This arrangement should always be placed in a modern container or a bottle; I do not think a Moribana container would do it justice.

Choose a perfect rose for your Shin and support it with a twist of wistaria or willow; or take a tall grouping of peach branches which form graceful arcs and curves and have their flowers close to the stem; for jushi use spiraea or some other delicate material with softly intermingling lines.

In this "Heaven only" arrangement Shin must be at an angle of 5°.

These few examples are sufficient to indicate the endless variety which can be achieved in the Free Style. You are encouraged to mix colours, use two or three types of plants in one arrangement, combine dried material with fresh, and seasonable with unseasonable. But remember that the principle of

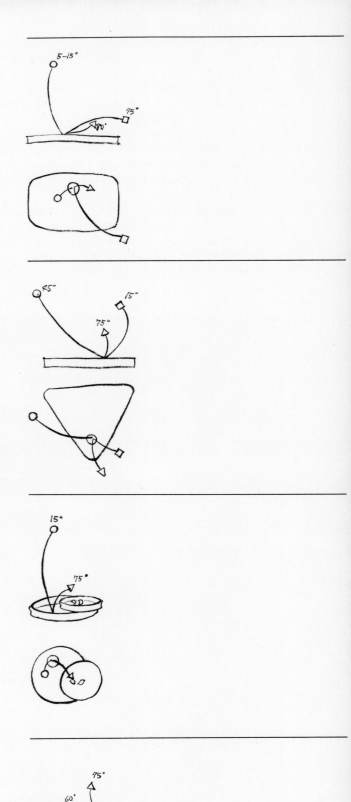

three must be adhered to; and, even though your arrangement may be fuller than your Natural Style ones, avoid overcrowding by creating space, and keep that tranquillity which is an essential part of every arrangement.

In the early days of your Free Style work make a point of using many more jushi in your arrangements. Take care with your angles. You cannot take a short cut by making a bad basic arrangement and calling it a Free Style one. Much of the character in Free Style comes from your more generous use of flowers. The preceding instructions concentrate on the use of branches and flowers. But beautiful Free Style arrangements can be made by using a variety of materials for your main lines, including roots, driftwood and dead branches. In these cases the outline of the arrangement would be made by branches, and the accents by points of colour. A mass arrangement of roots with driftwood crossing might appear flat, so that, to avoid this, instead of using a large piece of driftwood coming to the front, you would make an accent with a mass of flowers. The arrangement would still be flat, but looking at it from the front, your eye would meet a point of

accent. In this manner you can build up an enormous collection of roots and driftwood, so long as you make an accent with fresh flowers or masses of green to provide balance and contrast.

If you are using roots and branches without a container, you will need two or three points of balance at the base.

A Free Style root arrangement will be much bigger and heavier than the root variation mentioned in the Keishin Kei chapter. In the Keishin Kei variation the main lines are clearly stated. In Free Style we rely much more on mass and geometrical pattern. For instance, if you can find a fisherman's large basket with open crossweave to use as a container, try to pick up the pattern of the basket with an outline of criss-crossing branches; you must also keep the mass off centre, over one end of the basket. Again, if you use yellow willow coming out of a mass of roots, echo the colour of the leaf or branch at the base of the arrangement. The roots will act as a foil to the willow which will provide the movement; balance and unity will be achieved by carefully placed points of complementary or contrasting materials.

*Basic Free Style arrangement of Salix and Pink Sensation roses, in deep blue and brown salt-glaze stoneware container*

*Free Style arrangement in basic Moribana container.*
*Nylon reeds, Euphorbia fulgens and white lilac*

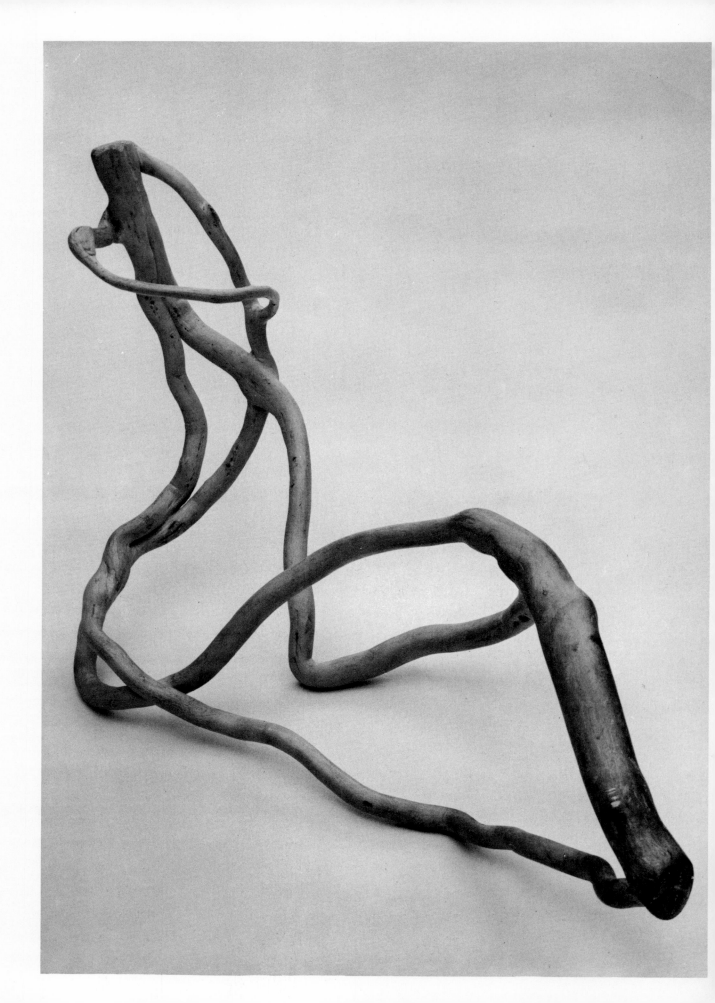

# *Chapter Eleven*

# Modern-Abstract and Avant-Garde, and Their Esoteric Differences

Modern Ikebana is an enigma to most Western flower arrangers. The lines are not clear, the meaning is elusive, and the materials are often non-floral.

In general, the answer to this lies in the development of modern art over the past ninety years or so. Ever since the French impressionists first broke with tradition, European painting and, later, sculpture, have moved farther away from pure representation towards the complete freedom of abstraction, surrealism and other schools. Eventually even the traditional raw materials of the artist underwent a complete revolution. For many centuries the only legitimate components of a painting were canvas (preceded by wood) and paint; the first collage, however, introduced all kinds of "alien" matter into painting, and today there are few objects under the sun, from plastic handles to twisted metal, which do not appear within a picture frame, or as part of a piece of sculpture.

Over the past forty years Ikebana, too, has undergone a similar change, moving from the traditional to the modern. The only point in which its development differs from that of other art forms is that while today no creative artist would attempt to paint in the style of Botticelli or make sculptures in the manner of Donatello, the flower arranger can, and does, do good creative work in both the traditional and modern idioms.

It is the complete freedom of modern art which explains why a modern Ikebana arrangement may consist of metal, glass, plaster, wood, silk, plastic or any other material you care to name, without containing a single flower or any plant material.

A brief glance at the history of Ikebana is sufficient to show that the modern style is a logical development from the earlier phases.

Rikka, the earliest formal style, used solely for temple arrangements, softened into Shoka (or Seika) which was less complicated, requiring fewer materials and smaller containers. Shoka, practised in the palaces and homes of noblemen, was less formal, with only three main lines, which made it more easily adaptable for everyday use in the Nageire and Moribana styles, suitable for the homes of commoners.

Nageire, the "thrown-in" style in a tall container, was more directly influenced by its predecessors. Moribana was adapted from earlier flat baskets, called kero, specially made to hold the piled-up lotus petals which were scattered at certain Buddhist ceremonies.

About 1900, Unshin Ohara, a famous flower master, adapted the idea of the earlier flower holders, called hanadome, such as the bunches of straw used in Rikka and the lead crab, and invented the shippo. He utilized the idea of the piled-up petals which, of course, needed no fixing, and the Moribana style was born. To celebrate this achievement, a Moribana monument was erected to him on Mount Rokko in Kobe. Mr Houn Ohara, the present Grand Master of the Ohara School, is the grandson of the famous Unshin.

*Modern arrangement*
*"The Engine".*
*Pampas grass is used as smoke,*
*pine as wind, and red carnations*
*as fire. Black stoneware*
*container made by the author*

*Opposite page*
*Modern arrangement of five*
*white arum (calla) lillies*
*their stems bound at the base*
*with bass to prevent curling.*
*Modern blue container*

*Abstract arrangement.*
*Painted branches of Aegle*
*sepiaria – orange cumquats –*
*and pale green okra pods, in*
*black Rosemary Wren container*

*Opposite page*
*Abstract arrangement.*
*Three looped willow branches,*
*berries of viburnum opulus and a*
*Bocconia cordata leaf, in a*
*salt-glaze stoneware container*
*by Denise Wren*

Moribana was the first style in which comparative freedom from the traditional rules was possible. Together with Nageire it served as the inspiration of the Modern Style.

This falls into two categories – Abstract and Avant-Garde. The Free Style, which is often called modern, has been described in its elementary phases in the previous chapter. As you will recall, a Free Style arrangement is primarily one of good design, but falling outside the basic patterns and rules of the preceding styles. For that reason I regard Free Style as an intermediate phase between the natural and unnatural use of material, and between the use of natural and unnatural materials.

For the sake of clarity let us bear in mind that a Free Style arrangement will necessarily be a modern one, but a modern arrangement need not be a Free Style one. A Rikka or Shoka may be a modern arrangement, though in either case the basic design must be observed, but with complete freedom of choice of material.

In Modern Ikebana success will only be achieved after the study and assimilation of the basic designs in the natural styles. Newcomers may find some of the extreme forms a little baffling at first; not so the diligent student who, having practised the earlier styles, has developed an eye for design.

In the preceding styles "what was left out was as important as what was put in". Now the maxim is: "It is not what is combined but how it is combined." The section of Ikebana presented in this chapter is the art of flower arranging in which few or no flowers are used, but an endless variety of other materials may be introduced. Sometimes one recognizes in a tree stump, a root, a lump of rock, or even a tangle of wire an actual or potential form or pattern which can be used in a design. A stone or a piece of driftwood may suggest a likeness to an animal or a bird which may form the nucleus of an arrangement, or stand alone. Try not to relate your finds always to natural subjects.

An abstract arrangement is one of geometrical form and design, bearing no resemblance to natural objects, and in which the arranger's ideas and taste dominate. Flowers, if any, are used for colour and texture, and branches for design. Awareness of the

nature of the material will enable and inspire the arranger to subordinate the branches to the required design.

Lines being of paramount importance, let us pause here to consider them as such, having already previously studied the lines of trees and flowers.

Lines are the main preoccupation and concern of the architect, artist and sculptor. We recognize buildings and sculptures by their outlines, and paintings by the pattern of their lines. Colour and texture also play a part, but it is the line which rules.

Lines stimulate our emotions and aesthetic appreciation. The elegant lines of a narcissus leaf, supporting the slender, straight line of the flower stem, give a feeling of great delicacy and purity. The iris with its strong, straight line is masculine; the peach branch with its beautiful curves is feminine. This is why we use soft curves if we seek to make a feminine arrangement, and thick, forceful lines for a masculine one.

Horizontal and vertical lines have little movement but great stability.

Slanting lines have movement but little balance, so they must be supported. Curves, used in moderation, can convey an air of gaiety. Finite or infinite curves

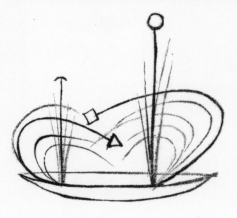

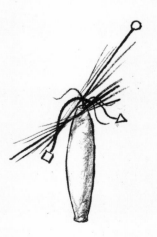

Opposite page
Abstract arrangement in a salt-glaze container.
Super Star roses with dried wistaria vines

can express movement, freedom and flexibility. Triangles, rectangles and, in particular, parallelograms, give good linear effects. The result of combining straight lines and curves can be seen on page 95, where the circles of cumquats, the curves of fresh okra pods, and the straight lines of the hardy orange, arranged in a bottle-shaped container decorated with horizontal circles, form an elegant unity. In the Abstract Style there are no rigid rules governing the lines such as there are in the natural styles, but the lines are of such vital importance that the arranger needs experience, judgement and aesthetic perception in placing them.

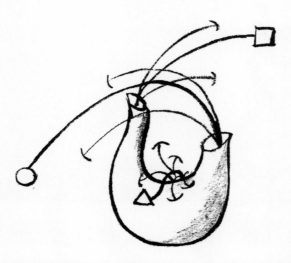

We are taught that although we should learn from the work of others, our aim is to create, not to copy, and therefore the following paragraphs contain mere suggestions.

Practise massing flowers and foliage, stripping branches and bending stems, and carry out the following Modern exercises in various styles. Choose medium-size modern style containers in simple designs. Some modern containers are so ornate and complicated that they should only contain a sparsely leaved, bare or berried branch. In many cases the complicated shape of the container dominates the entire arrangement. This is no new problem, for a long time ago the Emperor Meiji, celebrated for his sense of beauty, said in one of his poems: "Let us arrange a single branch of pine in a little vase that is painted with beautiful flowers", meaning that, if you have an ornate container, you must use plain material in it. A very intricate modern container is not suitable for a complicated arrangement.

In our first exercise in the Modern Horizontal Style, the two main lines, Shin and Soe, will go horizontally one to the left, one to the right. Use pine, bulrushes or any other material that has enough strength to carry its own weight when placed in the horizontal position. The choice of jushi to support the main lines is once again yours. Balance may be achieved by a bunch of massed flower-heads or leaves as Hikae, standing off centre in the opening of the container, covering the base of the stems which may be unsightly. Pay the utmost attention to form, line, colour, texture and space. These are the requisites of the Modern Style.

For the Modern Upright Style two diagrams are given: one for a flat, Moribana container, the other for a tall, modern one.

In the Moribana, Shin follows the zero line, standing erect. The supporters rise to Shin and cross in curves or at angles, perhaps accentuating the outline of the container. Soe is placed on the outside of these supporters. The arrangement is balanced at the base by Hikae, this being one or two clumps of differently coloured flowers, or one of flowers, one of foliage.

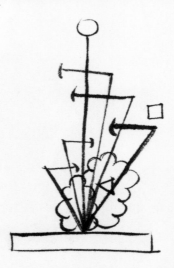

Generally speaking the flowers should be of the same kind but different in colour. If you wish to use greenery, choose tree foliage and, if necessary, clip it to the required shape. Flowers rarely have enough foliage of their own, and it is not a good idea to tie their leaves into a tight bunch, as they bruise very easily. Pine, yew and small-leaved trees, such as the cupressus, can be tied and clipped effectively. The second arrangement is made in a fairly plain modern-style container. Shin stands in the upright

*Opposite page*
*Abstract arrangement – pampas grass, Mimosa acacia and dried wistaria branch in black ceramic container*

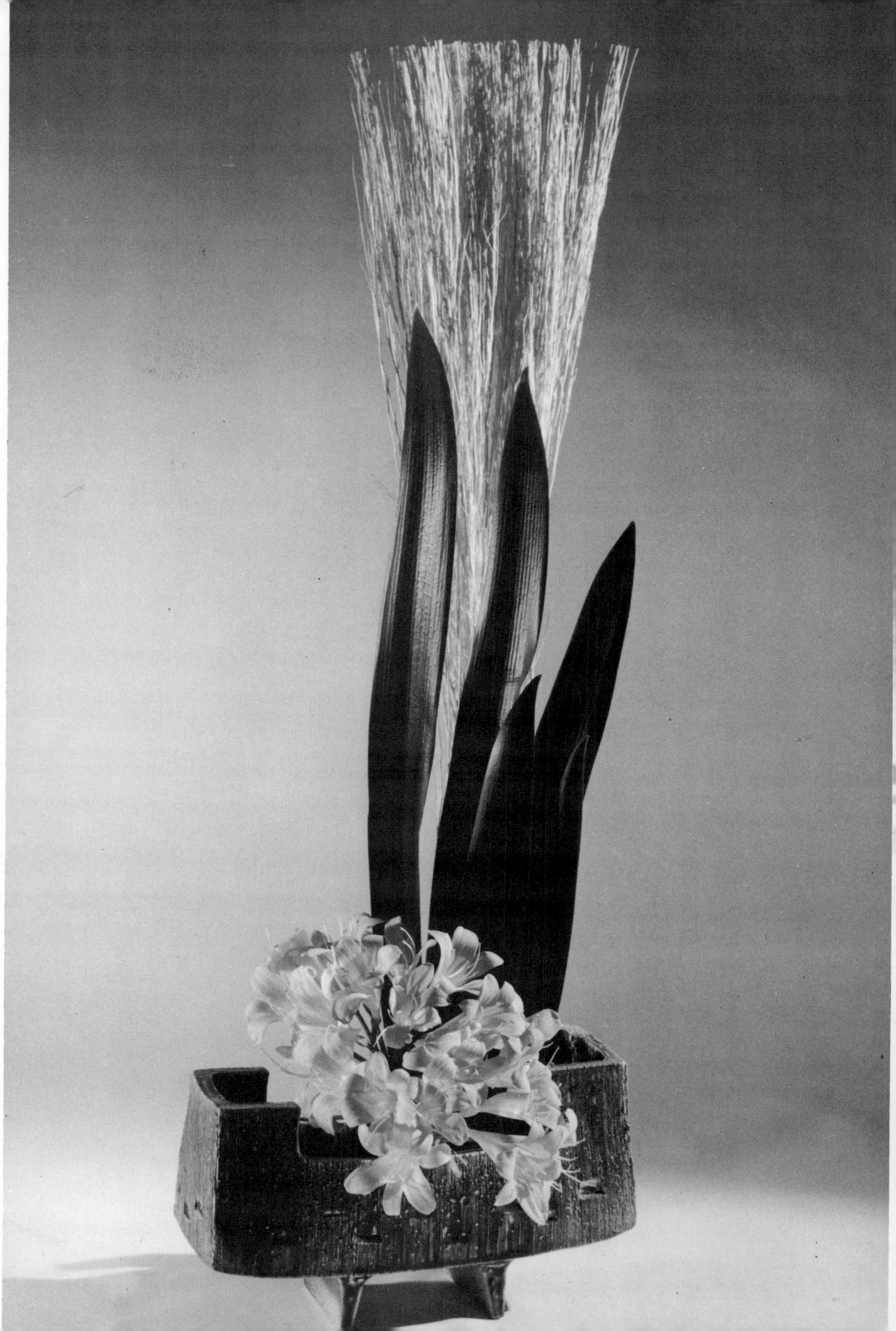

position. Support it with thin, straight jushi, and add a long, straight line of flowers from the neck of the container for about two-thirds of the length of Shin, in order to accentuate the upright line, the top one being Soe. Place a mass of flowers or foliage at the back as a "shadow", and soften the outline of the container's lip by bringing a leaf or single flower forward, as Hikae, so that it will obscure, without touching, a small section of the rim of the container. Some arrangements in the modern section are inspired by the seasons. Rain, for instance, is a very popular theme. Since rain falls, a tall container will often be used to allow the material to fall. Try bending reeds over carnations, barley stems over coloured glass, or monstera leaves over tulips. If you use heavy, brightly coloured summer flowers, spray

*Modern arrangement consisting of pink hyacinths, skeletonized magnolia leaves and soya seed-heads, in an oval black Japanese container*

*Opposite page*
*Abstract arrangement. Clivia flowers and leaves with dried and bleached summer cyprus in cinnamon-coloured container*

them with water to give the effect of dampness.
There are countless ideas for this rain arrangement –
Iris stylosa leaves over roses, or aspidistra leaves
split into fronds and bent over flowers – but do not
bend all the stems at the same point, stagger them
slightly.

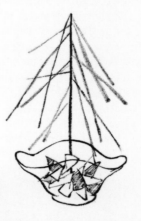

The abstract arrangement in the colour section is the
epitome of rain, using Mitsumata, driftwood and palm,
warmth and colour being added by the red velvet
poinsettia flowers. The basic structure is made of
sturdy wood which is then embellished by the red
flowers. The rain is made to cascade; single drops are
indicated by small sea-blue baubles.

Conversely, in an arrangement inspired by the
rays of the sun or the sunrise, lines will rise and fan
out as the rays do. For this theme use bright, hot
colours; try leaves of palm and marigolds, for
instance.

Whatever material you choose for your main lines –
this applies to every phase of Ikebana – let it dominate.
In Morimono, for example, it is the fruit which is
important; and if, in a modern arrangement, you wish
to use leaves for your main lines, it is the leaves
which are important, and the other material should
support them. Grasses are very light, but with good
design they can be made to dominate. Make yourself
forget the pretty individual faces of flowers in these
arrangements, which must be either bold and
colourful but never coarse, or delicate and gentle but
not insipid.

When giving a title to a modern arrangement – this
is sometimes unavoidable with exhibition pieces –
interpret its meaning broadly and leave some of the
pleasures of interpretation to the viewer. But please
remember that the arrangement must be able to
stand as a separate entity, without the title. "A Frog
in a Pool", for instance, could well be the title of an
arrangement, but you should allow the viewer's
imagination to supply the frog, don't add one.

*Modern arrangement of three red poinsettias and
two wands of natural coloured polystyrene "foliages"
in black container*

Avant-garde means new trends in modern design.
Design and texture are most important here. It is
possible, though rare, to find a piece of wood or rock
which could stand alone as an arrangement. But

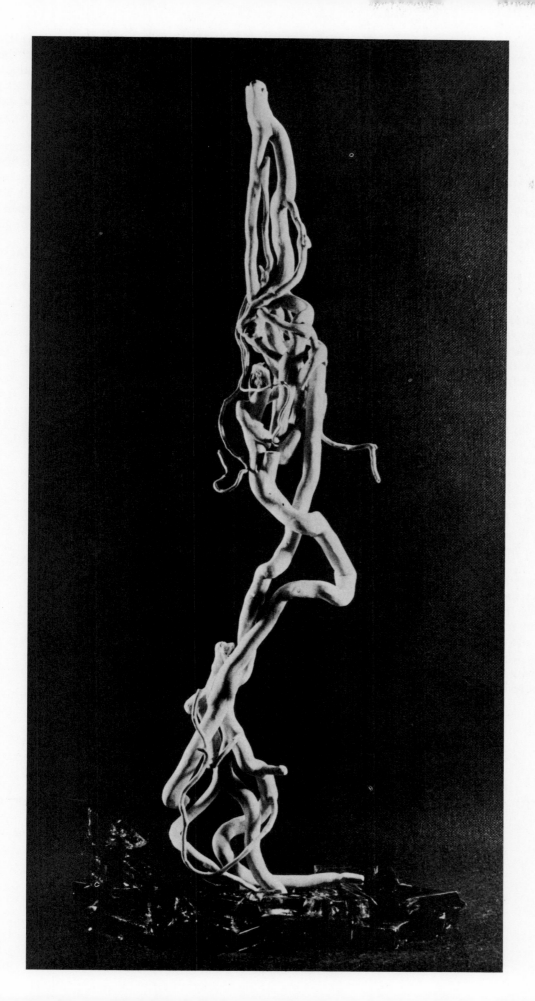

*Avant-garde sculpture
made of stripped, sanded
and waxed wood,
on a base of thick glass
in various colours*

even if one does succeed in this, hard manual work, patience and imagination are needed to cut – or shape – and prepare it.

For the two statues illustrated in this book, I obeyed the Sogetsu rule that one must seek out the material oneself, and looked for and found some ivy with which I could make an abstract shape, complicated in design yet expressing the softness of nature.

I selected the wood with great care. I kept it for about three days, waiting for the bark to shrink, and then stripped this from the wood with the knife from my tool kit; an old kitchen knife with a comfortable handle is also a very reliable tool for this purpose. For obvious practical reasons I surrounded my chair with a large sheet of plastic before starting on the stripping. I let my mind range over possible title subjects while doing this; the nature, shape or texture of the wood suggest and inspire design.

The next step was to trim and cut away all confusing and unwanted lines, to cut and rejoin pieces if necessary. To accentuate a curve or an angle, I bent the wood, tied it with bass which does not stain the wood, and finally left it to dry slowly over a period of 2 to 3 weeks.

The last step, sanding and smoothing, was the most tedious one. Having removed every scrap of pith, I rubbed the wood with very fine glass paper. If I consider that the shape is worthy of standing as a piece of statuary, I also rub the wood with pure beeswax. This must be done very carefully, too, because otherwise the beeswax may make yellow lumps on the wood. If the wood is to be used in conjunction with flowers and foliage, I waterproof it with a colourless, matt, water-repellent liquid, not with varnish.

Another avant-garde arrangement photographed is made of swarf, i.e. metal shavings which I obtain at the blacksmith's. These shavings should be handled with great respect, as they are very sharp, and also they should be held at arm's length and wrapped carefully when collected, because they will undoubtedly be covered in oil. This must be washed off if you wish to paint the material. Use a detergent and plenty of hot water in a large sink to do this. Rinse well, put it in butter muslin, shake off the excess moisture and dry quickly in a warm atmosphere. This is essential to avoid rust. If your shavings get rusty, you might just as well throw them out and start all over again, because you will never remove the rust without cutting your fingers badly.

Another source of infinite pleasure in the search for avant-garde materials is the glass or plastics factory. Cullet, the glass manufacturer's waste, is wonderful to use but very sharp; use it at your own risk and do not let students or children handle it. Plastic is very light and colourful. It lacks the lustre of glass, but gains in colour and lightness.

I suggest you try out a few of your ideas with, perhaps, nylon reeds, now available in many colours, or Mitsumata, the dried and stripped branches of edgeworthia. You will also find stems of angelica useful. This giant herb, which is easily grown from seed, has stems not unlike those of the bamboo. The giant cow parsley is another alternative. All these materials, which grow straight by nature, are eminently bendable when green. Dried, they keep indefinitely and can be put to many uses. In fact the possibilities are endless, just as in contemporary art. After all, Picasso's abstract of a dish-cloth with a hole in it, and a rusty nail, was exhibited at the Tate Gallery.

Several painters of today use techniques and achieve results which seem to me much more akin to advanced Ikebana than to the art of painting. Rex Dransfield's Lunarscape, for instance, made of pieces of wood, peach stones, cinders, ash and stones, as well as oil paints, would fit perfectly into the Ikebana reliefs described in Chapter Eight, and Rosemary Wren's rough salt-glaze mural would look quite at home in an Ikebana avant-garde exhibition.

No one can teach you to make an abstract or avant-garde arrangement. I can but try to guide your steps, in the hope that my hints will help you technically and inspire you with ideas of your own. The rest you must do yourself. I sincerely hope you will enjoy doing it.

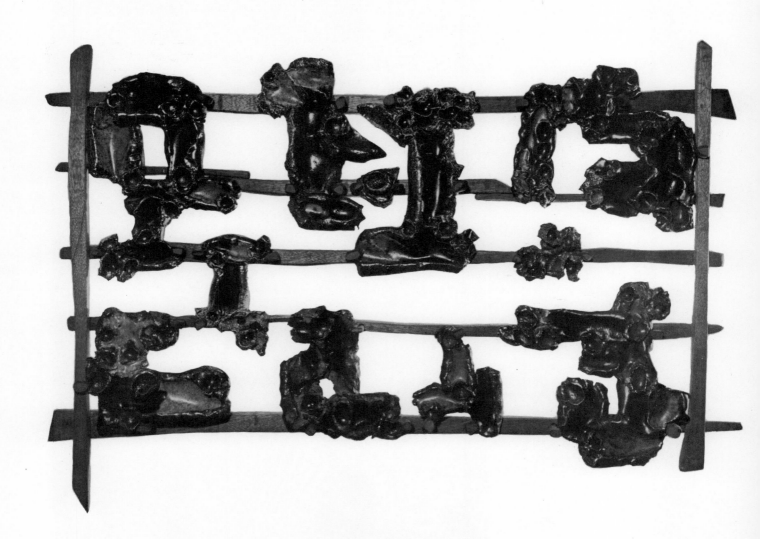

"High Fire"
Composition in salt-glazed stoneware and tile.
Pooled glazes in blue-green-grey colours
salt-glaze speckled brown; hardwood gingerish.
Fired to $1320°C$
by Rosemary D. Wren, A.R.C.A.

*New Year arrangement combines pine, larch, red and white chrysanthemums, and gold fan in a circular black container*

# Chapter Twelve

# Festival Arrangements and Their Folk-lore

Japanese tradition is rich in festivals. Most of them are of great antiquity, many have religious significance, but in the course of centuries all have become happy family occasions which are celebrated with colourful rituals and special flower arrangements, especially in country districts. The different districts of Japan have their own regional differences in dialect, calligraphy and custom, so that regionally these festivals are often celebrated in different ways, although their basic aims and ideas remain unchanged. In Ikebana diaries and calendars one often sees the photographs of arrangements that obviously have a story of their own. In this chapter you will find the descriptions and background stories of some festival arrangements which I hope will not only be of interest to you but will also add to your enjoyment, for it is much more rewarding to make an arrangement if you know the tradition behind it.

*January 7*
*Nanakusa, or the Festival of the Seven Herbs of Spring*
On this day the Japanese eat rice porridge and soup with seven herbs – parsley, shepherd's purse, cudweed, chickweed, Buddha's Throne, Chinese rape and radish. Traditionally these herbs are supposed to ward off all kinds of sickness throughout the following year.
Though they may not do so, there are two practical aspects which are undoubtedly beneficial. The time spent in the open air collecting the herbs in the fields or on the hills is well spent, and the temporary rest for the digestive system after the New Year celebrations, which in Japan are the cause of as much overeating as is Christmas in the Western world, is of great value.
The seven herbs are carefully washed and placed in a bowl in the centre of the table at which the family is sitting; they are then taken and eaten in the soup and porridge. For this reason no set arrangement is made. The herbs are arranged simply in a pleasing fashion, with great respect for cleanliness.
A sister celebration to Nanakusa is the occasion on which the arrangement of the Seven Grasses of

Autumn is made. It also is an occasion for family outings and long walks in the countryside to gather the seven "grasses" found at that time of year – Japanese clover, pampas, arrowroot, wild carnation, maiden flower, Chinese agrimony, and wild morning glory. Looking at the photograph of this arrangement, the Western reader may be surprised to find a chrysanthemum in this "grass" arrangement. This is because of the Japanese division of all plants into two main groups of "trees" and "grasses", with the latter including all flowering plants; this explains the presence of the chrysanthemum.
The Seven Grasses of Autumn is a classical arrangement, placed in the centre of a low, shallow container, or on a tray, in which case a well kenzan is used.
It can also be made in a basket.

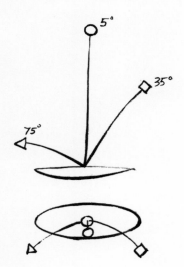

Hikae is the first main line to be placed on the kenzan, and it is the heaviest grass or flower of the arrangement. It is placed on the right or left front of the kenzan and projects just beyond the edge of the container, at an angle of $75°$. Soe is placed on the opposite side to Hikae, at $35°$ from the vertical.
Shin is placed on the centre back of the kenzan in an upright position, coming slightly forward, at an angle of $5°$, to the centre front.

Support Hikae with light jushi, but add a little weight at its base. Soe is supported by the secondary flowers, and Shin by light grasses, e.g. pampas and pampas leaves. By the side of this arrangement there are often found two small carved wooden dolls, called kokeshi, placed there to emphasize the country idea.

*February 3*
*Setsubun, or the Festival of the Change of the Seasons*
Setsubun, which according to the old calendar was New Year's Day, is also known as the bean-throwing (mame-maki), devil-chasing (oni-harai), and evil-dispersing (tsuina) festival. At least a thousand years old, this custom marks the end of winter and the beginning of spring, which is also regarded as a turning point in the fortunes of individuals. Traditionally, roasted beans are thrown in each room of the house, accompanied by the cry, "*Fuku wa uchi, oni wa so to,*" meaning "welcome, good luck, devils, out!" The children delight in picking up the beans. Later every member of the family eats one roasted bean for every year of his or her life, and one for the New Year.
There are also ceremonies at the temples when locally or nationally well-known people throw beans and small cakes wrapped in rice paper to those gathered in the gardens, who consider themselves fortunate if they catch them. In the country troops of men wearing lions' heads go round performing a humorous sacred dance to entertain people in front of their houses, chanting "*Fuku wa uchi, oni wa so to.*"
Our Setsubun photograph shows two masks, one representing wealth and happiness, the other the devil. The special arrangement for this day is made of holly or other prickly plant material, with a small fish speared on it. The evil smell of the fish is believed to drive away the devils, and the prickly leaves stop evil insects from entering the house. An alternative is to use a thorny plant and impale a small leek on it. The devil is reputed to dislike the smell, and the thorns stop evil from entering the house. In our photograph we used a paper fish with the holly, although the leek impaled on a thorn was a real one. There is also a small square box containing roasted beans.

*March 3*
*Hinamatsuri, or the Dolls' Festival*
Celebrated on the third day of the third month for the past thousand years or so, the Dolls' Festival is a very special occasion for small Japanese girls who regard it as their very own; it is the counterpart of the Boys' Festival on May 5.
Originally on this day people made simple paper dolls and wiped their bodies with them, symbolically removing all their sins and diseases, and then threw the dolls in the river. Subsequently the dolls became more elaborate, and the festival itself became an

occasion for parents to pray for the health and beauty of their young daughters.

Nowadays in Japan the Dolls' Festival is a gay and convivial occasion. Guests are served with sweets, white wine, puffed rice and white, pink, and green rice cakes. In the best room of the house the family's ceremonial dolls, which may be heirlooms or new acquisitions, are displayed in strict order on the steps of the hina-dan, a doll stand covered with red cloth. A complete set consists of fifteen dolls. At the top, the emperor and empress, resplendent in silk costumes, with three ladies-in-waiting. Lower down there are ministers, musicians and servants, all appropriately dressed. At the bottom there are miniature household articles such as a chest of drawers, crockery or musical instruments, and, finally, folding screens and vases with peach blossom.

The peach blossom, which in Japan opens in early March, is the symbol of feminine gentleness, softness and serenity, and also of happiness in marriage. For this reason the Dolls' Festival is sometimes called the Peach Festival.

In the traditional arrangement certain yellow flowers are combined with the peach blossom, as both bloom at the same time. The teaming up of yellow and pink is not, as a rule, pleasing to the Western eye, but we can keep the spirit of the arrangement and also achieve an attractive effect by using the palest possible yellow flowers.

*May 5*
*Tango-No-Sekku, or Boys' Festival*

On this day parents offer their thanks for the sound growth and development of their young sons and pray that they may have the manly virtues of strength and courage.

The day is also known as Flying Carp Day, or as the Festival of the Iris Flowers. Families with young sons set up a tall bamboo pole in their garden and attach to it colourful streamers and a huge red-and-black carp for each son, made of cloth or strong paper, with a hoop in its mouth to catch the wind. The house is decorated inside and out with iris flowers; iris leaves are used to scent the bath water. Rice dumplings, wrapped in fresh leaves, are served, with iris-flavoured rice wine.

There are two traditional explanations for the origin and symbols of this festival. According to one, on May 5, 1281, a Japanese prince offered special prayers to the spirits of his ancestors at the Fujimori Shrine, in the gardens of which the irises were in full bloom, asking for help against a threatened Mongolian invasion. On his return to the battlefield a storm arose and raged for three days. The invaders were scattered. Since then the iris has been regarded as a flower bringing good fortune, while its straight, sword-like leaves make it a clear symbol of bravery. The carp which swims up streams which are too rapid for other fish also stands for courage and for the determination to conquer difficulties.

The second, less heroic explanation is that in the old days farmers used to set up bright banners and grotesque, frightening figures in their fields to scare off the harmful insects which appeared in large numbers at the beginning of May. Later small replicas of these figures were made as dolls, representing infantry, cavalry, princes and heroes, and, with swords, armour and other tokens of war, were used to decorate the main alcove of the house in order to instil in boys respect for manly virtues.

The traditional flower arrangement for this festival consists of iris flowers and leaves only. In this country we can rarely buy the special "boys' iris", or Iris ensata, a Japanese variety which grows in sheltered places and is hard to find in shops even in Japan, so we must use one of the many kinds which are available here in May. We in the West do not, for our flower arrangements, differentiate between irises as strictly as they do in Japan, where it would be considered wrong to make the arrangement for the Boys' Festival with a species regarded there as feminine irises. By way of compromise, the traditional arrangement for the Boys' Festival has been illustrated not by a photograph but by a *sume* painting, which is perhaps the most beautiful way of all of depicting iris.

For this arrangement you will need a Moribana container and three kenzans. Two – preferably the two parts of a sun-and-moon kenzan – are placed to the left of the container, one behind the other; the third one stands at the right.

Shin is cut to the small measurement. It stands on the front kenzan on the left, supported by a minimum of three leaves in the front and three at the back. Soe, measuring three-quarters of Shin, stands on the second kenzan which is placed behind the Shin kenzan, and slightly to its left. It also is supported

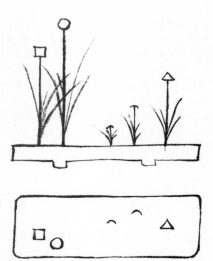

by three leaves at front and back which should intermingle with those of Shin to suggest unity.
Hikae, measuring three-quarters of Soe, stands on the third kenzan and is also supported by leaves.
All the flowers are upright.
Although iris stems are straight, the flower head is often at a small angle to the stem. You must ensure that this deviation is in each case to the centre of the arrangement.

## July 7

### Tanabata, or the Star Festival

This festival, commemorating the legend of Shokujo the weaver, and Kengyu the fisherman, is a charming way of spending a clear, warm summer evening with the family.

According to the legend, Shokujo and Kengyu were the devoted servants of the Lord who was so pleased with their work that He allowed them to marry.

The young people were delighted, but gradually they began to neglect their duties and spent more and more time in each other's company.

This made the Lord so angry that He separated the lovers, turned them into stars and banished them to either side of the Milky Way, the River of Heaven. On one night of the year only – on the seventh day of the seventh month – are they able to meet, but even then they have to ask the magpies to form a bridge for them across the River of Heaven.

Since the lovers can only meet on this one night, the romantically minded Japanese hope that the sky will be cloudless, and, to this end, children rise early to gather dewdrops. They mix these with sume to make ink, which has the magical property of making wishes written in it come true. They then write little prayers for a fine night, or poems, on pieces of cardboard, which are used to decorate the arrangement for Tanabata.

This is a kind of summer Christmas tree which is great fun to make in this country for a children's garden party. The Japanese use a bunch of bamboo branches, but as this is difficult to obtain in Britain, willow branches may be used instead.

Secure the branches in an upright position and decorate them with traditional paper shapes, cut and folded according to the rules of Origami and Kirigami. These shapes include a kimono, representing Shokujo, a boy's garment, representing Kengyu, a fishing net, a lobster and some fish.

There are also several magpies, a cormorant, a hare – for in Japan a hare, not a man, lives in the moon – and several beautiful festival baubles with long tassels.

Instead of string, pieces of coloured tissue paper are twisted into fine rolls and used to attach the ornaments to the branches.

*July 13-15*

*Obon (or Urabon-E), or the Festival of the Dead*

Dedicated to the ancestral spirits, this festival is a warm, hospitable annual event which the Japanese regard as an occasion for joy. It has been celebrated in Japan since A.D. 657, when it was first introduced from India.

For Obon, all the family go to the cemetery to tidy up the graves of their relatives, and make ready to receive their spirits in their homes for a day's holiday. A small bonfire of reeds is lit to welcome them and beautiful lanterns are hung in the house and garden. A feast of fruit, boiled rice and sweet cakes is laid out for them. There are also a horse and a cow, made perhaps from a cucumber and an aubergine on

which the ancestors may ride home. They return to the other world in a beautifully made seiryo-bune, or spirit boat. At the end of the festival this boat is laden with food and other offerings, and, bearing a burning candle, is floated down the river towards the sea.

*Arrangement for moon-viewing festival. Miscanthus grass, chrysanthemum, flower palm, laurel and grevillea leaves in a dark classical container*

## September 15

### Chu-Shu-Meigetsu, or Moon Festival

This autumn moon-viewing festival is also called Jugoya, which means "the fifteenth night". It is a traditional way of enjoying the beauty of the full moon on a pleasant, cool evening, which makes for a welcome change after the hot humidity of the summer months.

In the old days a splendid poem-making party was held on this night in the Emperor's Palace. Nowadays people sit and watch the serene full moon rising over their garden; they drink saki, eat rice dumplings round like the full moon, and compose poems. Special offerings to the moon are arranged in a simple way on small stands in the porch or veranda, and placed at twilight where the moonbeams will fall.

Traditionally these offerings are some fruits, dumplings and autumn flowers, and the custom, handed down from generation to generation, has become part of Japanese life and literature.

In the Moon Festival arrangement which we have photographed, the grasses represent the moonbeams and the pale yellow flowers the moon. This is a traditional arrangement. A classical version made with miscanthus and pale yellow flowers which bloom in the countryside at that time of year is sometimes used. By the side of this arrangement on a small stand fifteen rice dumplings are piled up in honour of the "fifteenth night".

### March and September

### O-Higan, or the Festival of the Dead

This week-long festival is held twice a year, at the times of the vernal and autumnal equinoxes when day and night are equal and the sun rises due east and sets due west. It is said that at these times the souls of the dead are particularly susceptible to the prayers, thoughts and wishes of those who have not yet crossed to the other shore (higan), the Nirvana of the Buddhists and the "ulterior ripa" of Catullus' lament for his brother.

The whole nation, from the emperor himself to the poorest peasant, visits shrines and offers prayers to the ancestors. Cemeteries are visited, and the graves are made tidy and beautiful with flowers. This is not a sad occasion, and often a feast is held there, although no meat is eaten. It is the custom to have ohagi, i.e. soft rice cakes covered with sweet bean paste.

The festival was first celebrated in 1043 by the Imperial Court and is still observed throughout the nation.

A simple, austere arrangement of white flowers, dead leaves and bare branches is usually made for this occasion.

### The Wedding Arrangement

This is a classical arrangement placed in the centre of a circular container. It is made up of an odd number of omoto – Rhodea japonica – leaves which are very green, very strong and long-lasting, representing the beauty, strength and longevity which, according to tradition, the Japanese man seeks in a wife. Omoto leaves are not obtainable in this country, but photographs of this arrangement appear so often in Japanese publications that it is interesting to know the story behind it.

In the absence of Omoto leaves I suggest those of the dracœna or aspidistra. The leaves are placed in a classical fashion, with the base compact, the leaves looking natural. The shortest leaf is placed to curve over a small bunch of berries, symbolizing the mother's arms folded over the future children of the marriage. The arrangement stands for strength, happiness, long life and many children to continue the family line.

*New Year Arrangements*

These fall into two categories, depending on whether they are placed outside or inside the house.

The outside arrangement which stands at every gate on New Year's Day consists of a pair of kado-natsu, or gate pines. These are upright arrangements, combining fresh, light bamboo with dark green pine branches. Sometimes the third "friend of winter", i.e. a sprig of plum blossom is tied into the bunch. The pine is strong and rugged, the bamboo straight and enduring, the plum pure and courageous, and therefore this arrangement expresses the hope that the New Year will bring vigour, steadfastness, long life and virtue.

Another arrangement, which hangs on the door, consists of pine and a small plaited ring of straw in the centre. Traditionally this reminds us of the story of the sun goddess who, having quarrelled with her brother, withdrew into a cave and plunged the whole world into darkness. She was eventually lured out by the sound of music and dancing which excited her curiosity, and a straw rope or shine-nawa was put across the entrance of the cave to prevent her re-entering it. This story accords well with the New Year when the days are beginning to grow a little brighter.

Pine and straw hung on the door means that the house is clean, and evil spirits are not allowed to enter.

The indoor arrangement we have photographed for the New Year includes the daidai, the bitter orange whose repetitive name suggests continuity, and kombu, a kind of seaweed whose name with a slightly changed pronunciation means a wish for joy and happiness. There is also a lobster which symbolizes long life, because in Chinese mythology its name was written as The Aged of the Sea. The leaves stand for humility.

All this is placed on top of two large cakes made of machi, which is steamed and pounded rice; the cake itself is called kagami-machi. Placed one upon the other, the smaller one being on top, the two kagami-machi are laid on two sheets of pure white paper on a little stand, and put in the tokonoma. When fresh, the kagami-machi are eaten with jam or honey; when they become stale, they are boiled. The custom is not to consume them until January 11, and to break them with one's hands instead of cutting them with a knife.

*Traditional New Year arrangement*
*features a lobster, an orange, seaweed*
*and rice cakes with two leaves of skeletonized fern*
*and fresh laurel on a classical base*

*The Cha-no-yu, or tea ceremony, is one of the most ritualistic of Japanese customs, its purpose being to encourage harmony in human relationships, aesthetic appreciation of beautiful things and periods of tranquil thought.*

*The custom came from China in the sixteenth century and was first adopted in Japan by nobles and warriors. A special room, a chashitsu, is built, usually about 10 feet square, separated from the main house by an immaculate tea garden, designed as a microcosm of nature, usually containing rocks, roots, trees, lanterns, and always a water basin. The short walk through the roji, or garden, is an important part of the preparation, for it is here that all connection with the busy and noisy world will be severed and one should be able to compose oneself and enter the chashitsu in a tranquil and receptive frame of mind. Inside, everyone is equal. Social and political ranks are not recognized*

*there and talk of business and politics is not permitted. Conversation is, therefore, about the arts and the beauty of nature. Etiquette is strictly observed.*

*The powdered green tea which is used is made from the new leaves of old plants which are specially tended and grown for this.*

*The photograph shows some of the personal items used in Cha-no-yu. The whisk made from finely split bamboo is used to mix the tea, and the bamboo ladle for water. The exquisite lacquered container holds the powdered tea; the handle-less cups are of individual design. The tea ceremony rules are extremely complicated, but, when analysed, are clearly meant to simplify and minimize the work, for it must be remembered that the most important part of the Cha-no-yu is not the making and drinking of tea, but the congenial atmosphere of harmony and restful talk with friends*

# Chapter Thirteen

# List of Plants Used in Illustrations

| | |
|---|---|
| *Aegle sepiaria* | Deciduous hardy orange. Slow-growing. Only suitable for warm soils with moderate frosts. |
| *Agapanthus umbellatus* | Perennial herb with short, creeping root stock and thick roots. Can be grown out of doors in mild areas, or kept in large pots and stood out in the summer. Needs much water in warm weather. |
| *Almond* | Prunus communis. Tree of 10–20 ft. with white or rose flowers and edible fruit. Hardy. |
| *Alnus glutinosa* | The common alder tree which grows wild in damp ground by rivers and streams. |
| *Alstroemeria hybrid* | Peruvian lily. Has fleshy, tuberous root. Resents disturbance. |
| *Alstroemeria aurantiaca* | Should be divided with care, or raised from seed and pot-grown. Most varieties are hardy in a well-drained, sunny position if planted at least 6–8 in. deep. |
| *Amaryllis* | South African bulbous plant with deciduous foliage. Needs fibrous loam with sand. Likes sheltered position at foot of south wall, or against hothouse wall. Hardy in the open in south-west England. |
| *Amaryllis belladonna* | The Belladonna Lily. Needs warm, sheltered position, well-drained soil. Dislikes disturbance. |
| *Anthurium andreanum* | Moisture-loving perennial, needs minimum temperature of 60°–65° in winter, 70°–80° in summer. Will survive at lower temperatures, but higher ones suit it better. |
| *Arum Lily* | Zantedeschia aethiopica. Also known as calla. Can be grown out of doors in warm areas, especially the Crowborough variety. In the greenhouse only needs frost-free treatment but will flower earlier with more heat. Easily propagated by planting young suckers in spring. |

| | |
|---|---|
| *Arum pentlandii* | Summer-flowering greenhouse Arum Lily. |
| *Arundinaria* | Bamboo. Hardy if given a sheltered position, with protection from north and east winds. Evergreen. Likes good loamy soil, hates drought. |
| *Asparagus fern* | Can be bought from the florist or grown in the house or greenhouse. Very easy culture. The best variety for a house plant is Asparagus plumosus nanus which grows to about 2 ft. It can be trained as a greenhouse climber. |
| *Azalea pontica* | Needs an acid soil. Has sweet-scented flowers and beautiful autumn colouring. |
| *Berberis* | Genus of deciduous and evergreen shrubs with prickly stems, most of them hardy enough for cultivation in England. |
| *Bocconia cordata* (syn. *macleaya*) | Plume Poppy. Herbaceous greenhouse plant, grows to 5–7 ft. |
| *Calla* | See Arum Lily. |
| *Camellia japonica* | Lime-hater. Needs light medium loam mixed with decayed leaf soil. Much hardier than generally supposed, but likes some light shade or a south wall to protect the flowers from the morning sun, should they be covered with frost. |
| *Carex paniculata* | Tussock-forming sedge, grows in ditches and near streams. |
| *Cedrus atlantica glauca* | Blue cedar. Useful evergreen tree, eventually very large, but slow-growing enough for medium-size gardens. |
| *Chaenomeles japonica maulei* | Maule's Quince. All varieties of this deciduous shrub are very easy to grow. On some soils it flowers better if grown as a hedge or against a wall. Needs heavy pruning. |
| *Chlorophytum elatum variegatum* | Very easy house plant, propagated by planting plantlets which appear on the flower stems after flowering. |
| *Clematis montana rubens* | Vanilla-scented deciduous rampant climber, with rosy-red flowers. |
| *Clivia miniata* | Bulbous plant with evergreen leaves. Needs minimum temperature of 45°–55° in winter, 55°–60° in summer. |
| *Codiaeum hybridum* | Croton. Evergreen shrub with striking ornamental foliage. Very susceptible to cold. Needs minimum temperature of 60°–75° in winter, 70°–85° in summer. |
| *Cortaderia argentea* | Pampas grass. Densely tufted perennial of easy culture. Likes deep loam and a sheltered position. C. pumila is an excellent dwarf form. |

*Modern arrangement using flowering blackthorn branches and Aladdin tulips*

*Free Style composition using Sansevieria trifasciata Laurentii,
lotus seed heads and twisted vine*

| | |
|---|---|
| *Cornus alba sibirica* | Deciduous shrub, grows to a height of up to 10 ft. Very hardy, thrives in any soil. |
| *Cycas* | Palm. For greenhouse or conservatory; can be kept in warm, sheltered outdoor spot from May to September. |
| *Eremurus bungei* | Herbaceous perennial. Hardy, but needs care in planting or moving, as it has thick, brittle, thong-like roots radiating from the crown. |
| *Erica arborea* | Tree heather, grows as shrub or small tree. Likes acid soil. Hardy only in southern half of England. |
| *Eryngium alpinum* | Sea holly. Hardy herbaceous plant, easy to grow in light, sandy, well-drained soil. |
| *Eucalyptus perriniana* | Will survive outdoors in warm soils if first pot-grown to a large size with a woody stem. Must be restricted in height until well established, as it grows very fast – 10 ft. a year – and may blow over unless well supported. |
| *Euphorbia fulgens* | Leafy shrub. Needs minimum temperature of $55°-65°$. Should be pruned hard in June to within 1 in. of base. |
| *Fatsia japonica* (syn. *aralia*) | Can be grown as a house plant, or makes a dramatic shrub in sheltered areas with only moderate frosts and winds. |
| *Forsythia* | Falls into two groups. (1) F. suspensa and its varieties which flower on new one-year wood and can be cut hard, and (2) F. intermedia spectabilis and its varieties which flower on second-year wood and must be pruned and picked by removing alternate branches. |
| *Freesia* | Easily raised from seed in light sandy soil, in sunny cool frame. Sensitive to draughts. |
| *Gerbera* | Deep-rooting plant, hates disturbance. Most available varieties are selected hybrids of G. jamesonii. Given a winter temperature of $45°-50°$, they can be grown in pots or beds in the greenhouse, and planted out for the summer. |
| *Grevillea* | Evergreen greenhouse plant. Likes peaty soil. May be placed in open air in summer, plunging pots in ashes. |
| *Griselinia littoralis* | Useful shrub for hedges in coastal areas. Needs light, rich loam. Will survive inland but may suffer frost damage. Good plant for picking, being yellow-green all the year. |
| *Helleborus viridis* | Very easy culture. Likes moist, rich loam. Seeds freely. Seeds sown at once germinate quickly, but when fully ripe and hard, take a year to do so. |
| *Helleborus niger* | The Christmas Rose. |

| | |
|---|---|
| *Hydrangea petiolaris (scandens)* | Rich green leaves, white flowers. A vigorous climber. |
| *Ilex* | Holly. |
| *Lapageria rosea* | Beautiful greenhouse climbing plant, not easy to grow. Requires a warm greenhouse (55°–65°F.). |
| *Larix* | The common larch. |
| *Laurel* | Aromatic evergreen tree. Hardy. |
| *Ligustrum ovalifolium* | Garden privet used as hedge or shrub. |
| *Lilium longiflorum* | Easy to raise from seed, flowers in about twelve months. Has several varieties and hybrids, e.g., longiflorum formosanum. Flowering can be staggered by sowing at intervals. |
| *Lilium speciosum* (syn. *lancifolium*) | Useful for the greenhouse, or planted in warm spots in the garden. Grows to about 4 ft. |
| *Magnolia grandiflora* | Evergreen pyramidal tree, grows up to 30 ft. Glossy-dark leaves, creamy-white fragrant flowers. |
| *Magnolia stellata* | Compact, slow-growing deciduous shrub, up to 10 ft. tall. Hardy but sensitive to frost. Likes soil mixed with peat. Best species for small garden. |
| *Mespilus germanica* | Medlar. Hardy deciduous tree, grown for its fruit. Height up to 20 ft. |
| *Mimosa acacia* | Evergreen tree, mostly tender in Britain. Florist's mimosa. |
| *Miscanthus* | Tall perennial grass with fan-shaped terminal feathery pannicles. Hardy. Best grown in borders. Thrives in any soil. |
| *Montbretia* (*Crocosmia*) | Not generally hardy. For best results lift corms in November and store in frost-free place. Needs good soil and a sunny position. |
| *Nephrolepsis exaltata cristata* | Excellent fern for indoor decoration. Thrives in cool rockery or near water. All its varieties are easy ferns for the greenhouse. |
| *Nerine bowdenii* | Autumn-flowering bulbous plant. Can be grown in the greenhouse, or in a sunny, well-drained border at the foot of a south wall. |
| *Orchid, cattleya* | Long, dainty sprays of flowers. Easiest type for small greenhouse. |
| *Orchid, cymbidium* | Tropical conditions required. |
| *Orchid, odontoglossum* | Needs a moist atmosphere. Minimum temperature 50°–60° in summer, 45°–55° in winter. Resting period December–February. |

*An Autumn arrangement of palm and berries*

*Variation Number Seven.* *Using three gardenias on an Iwata glass container*

| | |
|---|---|
| *Paeonia* | Peony. Herbaceous perennial. Most varieties are hardy. Grows in practically any soil but prefers a deep, rich one with some lime. Hates disturbance. |
| *Paeonia suffruticosa* | Tree Peony. Grows up to 6 ft. high, flowers 6 in. or more across. |
| *Physalis peruviana* | Cape Gooseberry or Chinese Lantern. Half-hardy and hardy perennial, flowering June–October. Likes warm, rich soil, sunny, sheltered position. |
| *Pieris* (syn. *Andromeda*) *floribunda* | Erect, rounded, evergreen shrub, good for acid soils. An even more dramatic variety is forrestii, with brilliant red young growth. |
| *Pinus insignis* (*P. radiata*) | Monterey Pine. Very quick growing, may reach height of 115 ft. Heavy branches. Not very hardy. |
| *Pinus silvestris* | Scots Pine. Fast growing, too large for most gardens. |
| *Polygonatum multiflorum* | Solomon's Seal. Easy herbaceous perennial for partially shaded beds. |
| *Poinsettia* | See Euphorbia fulgens. |
| *Protea* | South African evergreen shrub for cool greenhouse. May be placed outside during hot summer months. |
| *Protea* | Australian. |
| *Prunus avium* | Wild flowering cherry. Pyramidal growth up to 60 ft. |
| *Prunus blireiana* | Round-headed tree, grows up to 30 ft. Purple leaves, edible fruit. |
| *Prunus communis* | Almond. |
| *Prunus persica peregrine* | Peach. Can be grown as tree in warm, sheltered areas, or against walls, or in the greenhouse, according to climate. |
| *Prunus sargentii* | Early-flowering cherry. Has deep crimson foliage in early autumn. |
| *Prunus triloba florepleno* | Grows to 12–15 ft. Needs pruning immediately after flowering. Also used in pots for forcing. |
| *Pyracantha coccinea lalandei* | Firethorn. Can be grown as a shrub, or trained as a wall climber. Prune in February. |
| *Rhododendron* | Genus including some 500 species, among them azaleas. |
| *Salix daphnoides* | Large willow shrub or tree. |

| | |
|---|---|
| *Salix glandulosa setsuka* | Easy willow, roots easily in water, contorts better with hard pruning. |
| *Salix vitellina* | Golden Willow. Grows up to 65 ft. Long catkins. Chiefly planted for winter effect. Needs annual pruning back to produce thick young shoots. |
| *Salix repens argentia* | Wide spreading prostrate shrub with dainty yellow catkins. |
| *Sansevieria trifasciata Laurentii* | A house plant. |
| *Spiraea arguta* | Hardy deciduous shrub. Grows to height of 6–8 ft. Likes sunny position, occasional top dressing of manure. |
| *Strelitzia reginae* | Bird of Paradise flower. Needs minimum temperature of 55°–65° in winter, 65°–75° in summer. The leaves are useful, either fresh or dried, when they curl beautifully. Takes seven years to flower from seed. |
| *Symphoricarpos racemosus* | Snowberry tree. 8–10 ft. high. Very easy culture. Needs ordinary soil. Will grow in light shade but does not berry well in dense shade. Hardy. |
| *Syringa* | Lilac. Easy to grow in sunny position. Likes rich, moist, loamy soil. Needs cutting back after flowering. |
| *Taxus fastigiata* | Irish yew. |
| *Typha minima* | Slender, $1-2\frac{1}{2}$ ft. high reed mace. |
| *Viburnum bitchiuense* | Deciduous shrub with fragrant flowers. About 5 ft. tall. |
| *Viburnum fragrans* | Sweet-scented flowers appear in late winter on bare branches. |
| *Viburnum opulus* | The Guelder Rose. Deciduous shrub, 10–12 ft. tall. Bright translucent red berries. |
| *Wistaria* | The dried vines of this deciduous twining climber are very useful in arrangements. |
| *Zantedeschia aethiopica* | See Arum Lily. |

*Opposite page*
*Haishin Kei. A Nageire arrangement of climbing hydrangea and orange poppies using the verticle and horizontal fixing*

*Natural scene arrangement using camellia branches
and pale pink tulips*

# *Chapter Fourteen*

# Glossary

| | |
|---|---|
| *Ai-kugi* | Nail pointed at both ends, used to join Rikka branches. |
| *Ashirai* | Alternative term for jushi. |
| *Bonkei* | Tray landscape. |
| *Bonsai* | Potted dwarfed tree. |
| *Bonseki* | Miniature landscape made of stones and sand on lacquered tray. |
| *Chabana* | Flower arrangement used in tea ceremony. |
| *Cha-ire* | Tea caddy. |
| *Chajin* | Tea master. |
| *Cha-no-yu* | Tea ceremony. |
| *Chasen* | Bamboo whisk used in tea ceremony. |
| *Chashaku* | Green pot used in tea ceremony. |
| *Chashitsu* or *Chaseke* | Tea house. |
| *Chawan* | Tea bowl. |
| *Chûshô-bana* | Abstract flower arrangement. |

| | |
|---|---|
| *Dai* | Base or stand for vases. |
| *Defune* or *debune* | Outward-going boat. |
| *Dôwa kubari* | Metal ring for holding branches together in classical arrangement, such as Suiban, q.v. |
| *Fakana-michi* | Space between two groups in Variation No. 5. |
| *Fune* | Boat or junk. |
| *Furyu* | Appreciation of beauty, combining perfect and imperfect. |
| *Gyodô-ike* | Fish path – space between two arrangements in one container. |
| *Haishin Kei* | The Flat Style. |
| *Hakama* | Sheath of bulbous plant. |
| *Hakumi* | The art of regrouping flowers. |
| *Ha-mono* | Leafy plants used for their leaves rather than flowers. |
| *Hana* | All plant life, including small rocks, stones and wood. |
| *Hano-mi-yutu* | Excursion to view the flowers. |
| *Hasami* | Flower-cutting scissors. |
| *Hikae* | Third main branch representing Earth. |
| *Ichi-mo-kubari* | Cross stick in classical kubari fixing. |
| *Ikebana* | Living material in water. |
| *Ikebana Bijutsu-ten* | Ikebana exhibition. |
| *Imba* | Negative leaves in modern arrangement showing their backs to the viewer. |

*Slanting arrangement using Magnolia stellata
symbolizes the passing of Winter and the approach of Spring*

Suishin Kei arrangement
using Salix repens argentia and muscari

| | |
|---|---|
| *In* | Negative (female, passive, or Earth). |
| *Irefune* or *Irebune* | Homeward-going boat. |
| *Jushi* | Branch, flower or leaf supporter to main line. |
| *Kadai* | Four-legged flower stand used for classical arrangements. |
| *Kado* | Peace through flowers (flower road). |
| *Kago* | Woven basket. |
| *Kake-bana* | Wall arrangement. |
| *Kake-danaike* | Wall basket. |
| *Kake-ita* | Long, narrow board to hold certain wall arrangements. |
| *Kakemono* | Hanging scroll picture or calligraphy. |
| *Kaki* | Generic term for flower container. |
| *Kansui-ike* | Water-viewing arrangement. |
| *Keishin Kei* | The Slanting Style. |
| *Kenzan* | Mountain of needles, i.e. pinholder. |
| *Kenzan-naoshi* | Tiny tool for straightening needles of kenzan. |
| *Ki-mono* | Tree plants. |
| *Komi* | Alternative term for Ichi-mo-kubari, q.v. |
| *Kubari* | All kinds of wooden supporter used in classical arrangements. |
| *Kusa-mono* | Grass plants. |

| | |
|---|---|
| *Matagi-kubari* | Most common kubari twig used in tall container. |
| *Mazu-age* | Collective term for techniques used to preserve cut plants. |
| *Mi-mono* | Berry plants. |
| *Mizu-age* | Water-raising, i.e. stimulation of water-conductive cells of cut plant. |
| *Mizu-giri* | Water-cutting, i.e. cutting stem under water. |
| *Mitsumata* | Edgeworthia. |
| *Mono* | Plant. |
| *Moribana* | Arrangement in shallow container with kenzan. |
| *Morimono* | Arrangement of fruit, vegetables and flowers. |
| *Nageire* | Casual arrangement in tall container with no kenzan. |
| *Nagisai orai* | Sailing towards the beach. |
| *Naki-dai* | Scroll-ended wooden base placed under classical arrangements. |
| *Nana-kusa* | Seven herbs or grasses (spring or autumn). |
| *Nejime* | Small cluster of flowers in classical arrangement. |
| *Nemoto* | Length of branch from neck of container to point of division in classical arrangement. |
| *Niju-ike* | Arrangement in double-tiered container. |
| *Ohina-sama* | Festival of Dolls. |
| *Oki-orai* | Sailing in the mist. |
| *Oki-fune* | Boat at anchor. |
| *O-shogatsu* | New Year. |

*Modern arrangement in the Upright Style*
*using Salix glandulosa setsuka and Australian Protea*

*Classical arrangement   Waning moon
using tulips and Hydrangea petiolaris*

| | |
|---|---|
| *Rikka* or *Rikkwa* | Ancient classical standing style. |
| *Risshin Kei* | The Upright Style. |
| *Ryôsô-ike* | The two-window arrangement. |
| *Snseei* | Teacher. |
| *Shibui* | Refined, subtle simplicity. |
| *Shikebana* | Branches placed on table without container. |
| *Shin* | Longest branch representing Heaven. |
| *Shin-no-hana* | Flower used in worship of Buddha. |
| *Shippo* | Heavy lead flower holder. |
| *Shi-sui* | Dead – stagnant – water (flower-arranging term). |
| *Shogi* | Translucent sliding panels. |
| *Shoka* or *seika* | Simpler classical arrangement. |
| *Soe* | Second longest branch representing Man. |
| *Sogetsu-kei* | Grass Moon School. |
| *Suiban* | Shallow dish used for sand garden. |
| *Suiriku-ike* | Land and water arrangement. |
| *Suishin Kei* | The Hanging Style. |
| *Suna-bache* | Shallow dish used for horizontal Rikka. |
| *Sung-iri* | Simple cylindrical bamboo dish. |

| | |
|---|---|
| *Tabi* | White sock worn with Japanese sandals. |
| *Tanabata* | Star Festival, held since 1629 on seventh day of seventh month. |
| *Tatami* | 6′×3′ straw matting used as floor covering in Japanese homes; mat placed under arrangements in tokonoma. |
| *Tango-no-sekku* | Boys' Festival. |
| *Tokonoma* | Shrine-like alcove in main room of Japanese home. |
| *Tomeki* | Another word for komi, q.v. |
| *Tomari-bune* | Ship in port. |
| *Tsuri-bune* | Hanging boat arrangement. |
| *Tsukimi* | Moon viewing. |
| *Tsuru-mono* | Vines used in hanging arrangements. |
| *Tsuyo-mono* | Classical category for plants which are weaker than tree plants and stronger than grass plants. |
| *Ukibana* | Floating arrangement. |
| *Usubata* | Special container for classical arrangements. |
| *Wabi-cha* | Complete harmony, chaste simplicity. |
| *Yo* | Positive (male, active, sun). |
| *Zen'ei-bana* | Avant-garde Style. |
| *Zori* | Japanese sandals. |

*Ikebana is the art of arranging flowers in containers.*
*Standing in front of me there is an arrangement*
*which I should like to describe.*
*It has been created with three kenzans.*
*The flowers are irises. The kenzans are*
*placed triangularly in a large shallow white*
*dish. The kenzans are different sizes.*
*Around these, little stones, mostly round ones,*
*have been placed. It is really an art to*
*create something like this.*
*I find the old Japanese art of arranging*
*flowers wonderful.*

*Ellen Siemokat*
*aged nine*

*Boat at anchor arrangement
using Super Star roses*

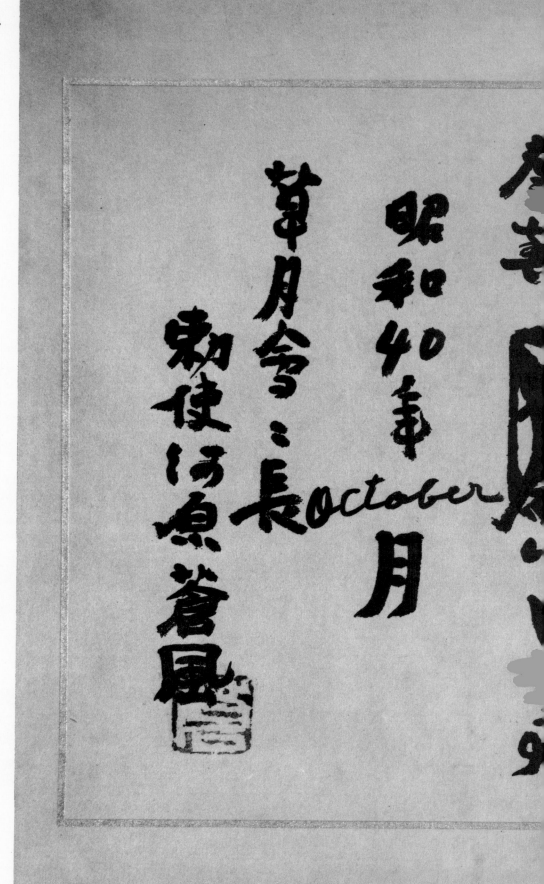

142 *Grade 1
Teaching Certificate
awarded to the author
by Mr Sofu
Teshigahara in 1965*